Reclaiming
African History

Through the voices of the peoples of Africa and the global South, Pambazuka Press and Pambazuka News disseminate analysis and debate on the struggle for freedom and justice.

Pambazuka Press – www.pambazukapress.org

 A Pan-African publisher of progressive books and DVDs on Africa and the global South that aim to stimulate discussion, analysis and engagement. Our publications address issues of human rights, social justice, advocacy, the politics of aid, development and international finance, women's rights, emerging powers and activism. They are primarily written by well-known African academics and activists. All books are available as ebooks.

Pambazuka News – www.pambazuka.org

 The award-winning and influential electronic weekly newsletter providing a platform for progressive Pan-African perspectives on politics, development and global affairs. With more than 2,500 contributors across the continent and a readership of more than 660,000, Pambazuka News has become the indispensable source of authentic voices of Africa's social analysts and activists.

Pambazuka Press and Pambazuka News are published by
Fahamu (www.fahamu.org)

Reclaiming
African History

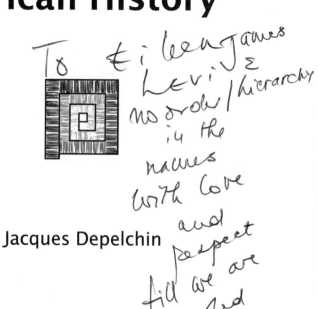

Jacques Depelchin

Pambazuka Press
An imprint of Fahamu

Handwritten inscription: To Eileen James & Levi — no order/hierarchy in the names — with love and respect till we are finished with capitalism. Jacques. Berkeley, August 7, 2011

Published 2011 by Pambazuka Press, an imprint of Fahamu
Cape Town, Dakar, Nairobi and Oxford
www.pambazukapress.org   www.fahamubooks.org   www.pambazuka.org

and

oozebap
Barcelona
www.oozebap.org

Fahamu, 2nd floor, 51 Cornmarket Street, Oxford OX1 3HA, UK
Fahamu Kenya, PO Box 47158, 00100 GPO, Nairobi, Kenya
Fahamu Senegal, 9 Cité Sonatel 2, POB 25021, Dakar-Fann, Dakar, Senegal
Fahamu South Africa, c/o 19 Nerina Crescent, Fish Hoek,
7975 Cape Town, South Africa

oozebap, PO Box 9142, Barcelona 08080, Spain

The English edition of this collection first published in 2011
The Spanish edition first published in 2010

Copyright © Pambazuka Press 2011

British Library Cataloguing in Publication Data
A catalogue record for this book is available from the British Library

ISBN: 978-1-906387-98-3 paperback
ISBN: 978-1-906387-99-0 ebook – pdf

Printed by National Printing Press, Bangalore, India

Contents

Introduction   vii

1   Taking African history seriously as a pre-condition
to healing humanity   1

2   In solidarity with Cité Soleil/Site Soley in Haiti   18

3   The routes and possibilities of a South–South subversive
globalisation: Africa and Brazil   33

4   Erosion of freedom: from Haiti to South Africa   43

5   Fear of emancipatory history in the DRC: from Kimpa Vita
to Lumumba, to the women of Panzi   48

6   Hungry for a voice: the food crisis, the market, and
socio-economic inequality   54
Co-authored with Diamantino Nhamposa

7   From Africa to Haiti to Gaza – fidelity to humanity   75

8   Born out of genocide; born to live off genocide   81

Afterword   90

Index   93

These essays are dedicated to:

My late parents:

Suzanne Nyabyinshi Depelchin (1921–1960) and Robert Depelchin (1908–2006)

Who brought us up safe, sound, whole

through predatory splitting times

My siblings:

Jean, Louis, Anne-Marie, Monique, Thérèse, Raymond

Who kept me whole

When in the hole

Kaidi, Chadi

Our children

Pauline Wynter

My life companion

Who inspired me

Peacefully, patiently, persistently

To keep going

letting go

of the ego

Introduction

These essays were first published in the online newsletter Pambazuka News. They are presented here in the order in which they were published, with the exception of the first one, which is meant to be introductory. This essay attempts to explain how history could be written in a way which would help break the mould and free African history from being implicitly hostage (conscious and unconsciously) to European and US historical intellectual frameworks. However, the essays can be read in any order.

All of the essays have sprung from one preoccupation: to demonstrate that African history is multiple in the sense that within it and through it, it is possible to reconnect to all the histories of those who have been disconnected. This reconnection to humanity is only going to be possible if through African histories one can understand the histories of the poor, the histories of Haitis, Abahlalis. In short the histories of all those who have been railroaded into looking at their own histories through a shattered looking-glass, deliberately and forcefully crushed so as to render the exercise impossible.

The histories of Africa and Africans will have to be understood in all of their complexities, from Haiti to Gaza, from the favelas, *bidonvilles*, shackdwellers, where the toilers of the universities and social laboratories of the future are reconstructing, healing humanity under the most inimical circumstances. Within these essays can be found, also, but so far, dimly, the idea that 'reclaiming' is not just for the sake of Africa, but for the sake of those who did everything to bury African history.

Jacques Depelchin
Salvador, Bahia, Brazil
April 2010

1

Taking African history seriously as a pre-condition to healing humanity

15 June 2009

My book *Silences in African History: Between the Syndromes of Discovery and Abolition*, published in 2005, ended with an epilogue in memory of Ken Saro-Wiwa and his companions. At the end of this introduction to essays which have appeared in Pambazuka News, we shall revisit the Niger Delta as a way of continuing to honour, remember and stand up for those who went beyond words in order not let go of fidelity to humanity. This is not an introduction as such; it is more a continuing search to find a way of expressing that which needs to be expressed in order to respond to the emergency we face.

Over the last months, the so-called financial crisis (see the explanation below) has reinforced the following conviction: capitalism has unleashed, sometimes knowingly, sometimes unknowingly, the most lethal machine in the history of humankind. The destructiveness of this machine – it should be called a mindset – cannot be ascertained because it resides in the conscience or consciousness of humanity. The genocidal system referred to in one of the essays has split, fragmenting the conscience of humanity in a manner that is reminiscent of how the splitting of the atom is most commonly and graphically rendered by physicists. This splitting of the conscience of humanity can be hypothesised as being similar to the conquering processes at the heart of capitalism's progression: systematic, relentless division to the point of generating other elements or, to put it more brutally, destroy that which created it. Destroy humanity and replace it with robots. From this process it is possible to say that, contrary to histories (critical and non-critical) of capitalism, things have gone from bad to worse. If that assertion is true, one should be able to say, as I have heard an old person say here in Salvador, Bahia, that most of humanity today is worse off than most of humanity was during Atlantic/Oriental slavery.

At the root of the above affirmation (which could be called an axiom) is an understanding that when crimes against humanity go unacknowledged, the consequences of such a denial open the way for bigger more massive crimes against humanity, in the same manner that a thief who gets away with impunity will be tempted to be more daring at his next attempt. A conscience deadened by crime, decriminalisation of crimes and criminalisation of its unwanted victims can only beget a dead conscience. The unwanted victims are many, unwanted because they have resisted, denounced the criminal system for what it is. The unwanted are the descendants of those who were enslaved either by the system and/or individuals and/or structures which promote discrimination based on religion, cultural beliefs, gender, race or physical appearance. Some of the ideological certainties which emerged in the process of resistance and denunciation contain lethal elements which must be avoided if healing processes are to be successful.[1] Might the following invocation help in such a process?

To heal from a history of the world
Built by selves decreed non-existing
Is to face such a history
Fearlessly, persistently, patiently
Facing a history of the world
Built by selves decreed invisible
Is to face such a history
Without fear, without shame
For fear and shame pain
The conscience afraid and ashamed
Of facing the ones they had decreed
Worthless for their worth is
Incalculable

And not just because incalculable
Has been the generated wealth
Facing such loss with dignity and respect
Is the call of a history calling for self respect
Dignity, serious, relentless dedication
To the task of healing the most wounded
The bloodsuckers, the genociders, the genocided
Freed from vengeance
Freed from violence
Freed from habits imprinted
Through torture
Through crimes against humanity
Healing from such an unacknowledged crime
Repairing it creatively away from
Humanitarianist charity
Toward solidarity
Will require extraordinary
Change of mind away
From the deified barbarism of so-called
Market laws and its lethal
Judicial, political, cultural, religious
Advertising industries and accessories
Taking one's history seriously
Could help, if taken seriously,
Heal the conscience of a world
Which has lost its mind seriously
Determined to recycle barbarism
Saying seriously no to barbarism
Has echoed through centuries
From Kimpa Vitas
Boukmans, Zumbis, Geronimos,

Beloveds, MLKs, Nehandas,
Generic sisters and brothers
From all corners of the Planet
The task has not changed
But tired limbs, minds and souls
Pacified us into doubting that
Maybe, just maybe
Those healing echoes were wrong
Maybe interference made us hear it wrong
Thinking that might is right
Might be the best way to move ahead
Moving ahead without looking back
At who is left behind
How much blood it has cost
Convinced the genociders of their triumph
Hiroshima and Nagasaki were not repeated
But how do we tell
Worse from better
Black rain from acid rain from regular rain
Mushroom cloud from a regular one
Preventing us from
Seeing, feeling how much worse
It has really been
Waiting for the aftermath
Cloud to clear to
Know if we are headed
Toward the end of humanity
Or its awakening
Uttering the same words
Heard over and over
From one crime to the next

How can human beings
Inflict such sufferings
Onto other beings
Still not heard
Refused to be heard
Because not couched
In the latest Columbus language
And, worse, not uttered
By a certified discoverer

I write this introduction in the context of what has been called a financial crisis (the latest Columbus language). Initially, that is not what it was called. There have been different names: credit crunch, credit crisis, liquidity crisis, food crisis, etc. From the very beginning there was also a discussion as to whether this was just yet another bubble like the ones which occurred earlier. In addition, questions kept being raised about whether this was a recession, how deep it was going to be and, ultimately whether it was going to be like the 1929 crisis, that is will the word 'depression' have to be used?

What was common to all these discussions was a reluctance to search deeper than the last few years for what could have been the cause of this crisis. Indeed, analysts were not interested in digging deeper than necessary. The hypothesis being used for this essay is that this crisis is more serious than anything which has been witnessed over the last 500 years. Furthermore, it might be helpful, at this juncture, to look back 5,000 years to gain a better perspective of how, why and where humanity went wrong.[2] What is being asked here is what would it take to pull back from the brink?

For this question to be answered fully two steps are essential. The first one is the necessity of questioning the politically and ideologically dominant frameworks or mindsets which are forced onto the way all histories are scripted, particularly with regard to capitalism. The vagaries and murderous divagations of the latter (i.e. capitalism) have been presented as the only possible spinal cord holding everything together and making sense of everything. Such presentations or affirmations end up becoming truths or, to be more precise, truisms. Having become the incarnation of capitalism and all that is positive about it, a single country (and its most powerful allies) has appropriated the mantle of all that is good and therefore has become the self-appointed watchdog of world security. The second one, a consequence of the first, is related to how African history is usually framed (exceptions do exist) as if it is a minor replica of the larger, dominant and dominating histories. This essay assumes that unless African history is reconsidered (taken seriously) from the perspective of the duty to heal humanity away from all the known practices of the victors, then humanity will indeed continue its march toward self-annihilation.[3]

It is almost as if a history (aimed at taking itself seriously) which moves away from 'the' model of all histories frightens, in and of itself, especially if the process of looking back might put into question certainties which have been expressed in various ways, but which could be synthesised as follows: 'We (the US) are the best, we have never done anything wrong, evil is always on the other side, the market is always right, might is right, as the most powerful nation we have the divine right to lead the rest of the world, we know best how to build democracy, our political system is the best of the world, our national security is sacrosanct even if its maintenance threatens the security of humanity. So be it.'[4] Since the end of the Second World War (WWII), the USA has publicised and implemented these slogans in a variety of ways, from the use of extreme violence to the use of the 'softer' strategies and tactics of winning hearts and minds. But the goal has never changed: achieve total and complete domination of the Earth and the space above.

When the atomic bombs were dropped on Hiroshima and Nagasaki on 6 and 9 August 1945 they signalled quietly yet massively and unambiguously what was meant to be the beginning of a new era, but which, really, was the continuation of a crime against humanity on another scale. That era, how it was entered, how it was announced, how it was described and what it ended up being has not really been understood to this day. In the most crude way, the dropping of the atomic bombs on Japan (and not on Germany) was meant to punish the Japanese not just for Pearl Harbour (which it was), but also to show any future offender how it would be treated. That it was a crime against humanity did not really matter to President Truman and his advisers. What mattered most was to show who was in charge and what would happen to anyone who dared to challenge that assertion.

How should the lessons be drawn? By whom and for whom?

More importantly, the mindset which led to splitting the atom and then atomising segments of humanity had been at work long before the physicists embarked on studying and building the most powerful weapon of mass destruction. Mass destruction had already taken place through what was described as discovery and then slavery. That destruction and what it did has still not been understood fully: the splitting of humanity, its consciousness and its conscience. This splitting process has not stopped. It has intensified, but how this has taken place has been hidden from view. It has, instead, been presented as 'progress'. Progression it certainly has been, but if it has been toward intensified destruction of life, then might regression not be a more accurate term? The arsenal at the disposal of the dominant mindset is much more than the weaponry: it encompasses in different degrees all the fields of knowledge and the arts (or what is left of them), including the art of living. In the art and science of forcing those who disagree to agree, torture has assumed increased importance.

Commenting on torture as practised by the US, Noam Chomsky drew attention to the fact that torture in the US actually has a much longer tradition than most US citizens would believe.[5] Among the reasons which led to a cleansing of the US historical record is the notion of 'American exceptionalism'. To some, such as the British journalist Godfrey Hodgson, this is just a myth; to others, such as columnist Roger Cohen, the US was born out of an idea, like a 'city at the top of a hill'. Chomsky then traces this idea to one John Winthrop who had coined it in 1630. With the idea of a city on a hilltop was born the idea engraved in what became the official seal of the colony of Massachusetts Bay, portraying an Indian with an inscription on a roll of paper coming from his mouth with the following words: 'Please come and help us'. It is not difficult to imagine what an indelible imprint an image like that has left on the minds of American citizens, generations after generations: a deep-seated conviction that, from the days of the British colonisers, Americans, like all colonisers, saw themselves as benevolent humanitarians. In conclusion, Chomsky refers to this process of historical cleansing as historical amnesia, and describes it as dangerous not just because it undermines moral and intellectual integrity, but – more importantly (in my view) – because it creates the bases for future crimes. Following from this point, what would happen if the current financial crisis were discussed in the media as the unfolding of a crime which has its roots in how the US became the wealthiest nation in the western world? In terms of the lives it has affected and continues to affect, aren't there reasons for thinking along the lines of a crime against humanity, precisely because the guilty, as has just be seen, will fight tooth and nail to continue appearing as benevolent humanitarians.

Structurally speaking, and at the risk of being repetitive, they want to be seen as those without whom the financial crisis cannot be resolved. It took a few centuries for Columbus' 'discoveries' to be contested and called something else. Hopefully, it will not take centuries to contest the naming of the current crisis as financial and focus, instead, on how this crime came to be prepared and committed – with the apparent consensus of many of its victims. A crime against humanity does not always have to contain elements of previous crimes. Hiroshima may not be Auschwitz, but it could be called its modernisation.[6] As such, it has opened the way for bigger crimes, perpetrated not so much by nuclear scientists as by financial engineers who invented profiteering instruments beyond the imagination of Wall Street managers.

Historians have debated the issue ad infinitum from all possible angles except from the one which would have put the US on trial in Nüremberg. Since the actual trial was organised, structured and conducted by the victors, that was an impossibility. It has been said that the bombs were really meant for the Soviet Union, to demonstrate to its leaders that the US would not hesitate to use the weapon against any of its future enemies. Yet, such rationalisations fail to deal satisfactorily with the question at hand: was it acceptable to resort to a crime against humanity in order to bring to an end a war which had known what came to be called the Holocaust?[7]

From the perspective of US leaders and their allies, the lessons from the post-WWII 20th century have been spelt out as brutally as they could be: the US and Israel do not belong to the international community; they dictate what constitutes the international community. Any country which is perceived as being opposed to their objectives will be dealt with in the way the innocent inhabitants of Hiroshima and Nagasaki were treated. Nothing, since then, can be shown to contradict this assertion. What has been sought by this policy is to ensure that the dying will always happen on the other side, and that anything which is perceived (and/or framed) as a threat will be treated with such extreme violence as to discourage any attempt to imitate it.

In a narrative of the 20th century, which starts with the winning of WWII by the USA and its allies, it might sound incongruous to refer to the USA as the perpetrator of a crime against humanity. Yet, if humanity is going to heal itself from such contradictory and politically/ideologically motivated denial, this recognition will have to occur, and the faster the better. What should be done once such a recognition occurs?

On May 2001, France, one of the enslaving and slave trading nations, declared slavery a crime against humanity, but implementing such a declaration has been more than problematic. The declaration, also known as la loi Taubira, for the legislator responsible for its drafting and passing in the French National Assembly, has run into stiff opposition from well-established historians such as Pierre Nora, who are offended at the idea that history could possibly be written by legislators.[8] Declaring slavery a crime against humanity might be more easily approved of if it were realised that it was that crime which opened the way to more horrendous crimes.

The attitude of the citizens of the world might be more attentive to current crimes if they could see the connections between past unacknowledged crimes. Historians of the victorious side have been a law unto themselves and it is understandable that they should protest when they are challenged through legislation by the descendants of those who had to suffer the unfolding of the crime. Throughout the process, from passing the law to when it becomes law, resistance has been fierce and continues to be so. For the generic winning side, which has always been right, has

9

always won, recognising that it has been wrong and thus facing the fact that the era of always having been victorious may be coming to an end, appears at first impossible to accept.[9] The more so when it begins to appear that what was wrong was not just the national politically-based narrative, but also its economic and financial basis.

To declare slavery a crime against humanity in a country which has enshrined the remains of Napoleon Bonaparte in the Pantheon in Paris might appear, at first sight, to be a betrayal. Napoleon, besides other slaughters all over Europe, also restored slavery after it had been abolished by the Convention. The manner he did it, led Claude Ribbe to describe him as Hitler's precursor.[10] Revisiting and reassessing French history will have to go beyond 1789. Atlantic slavery, how it unfolded and the wealth it generated for those who most benefited from it has built around it a sort of 'no trespassing' zone. It is something which happened and there is nothing which can be done about it. However, by labelling it a crime against humanity the 'no trespassing' label is removed and leaves it open for discussion. But the French legislators thought that they could pass the law by specifying that this crime against humanity did not imply the juridical obligation for reparation, but only a moral duty to remember, thus lessening, in their view, the impact of the law (Sala-Molins 2007:x).[11] Sala-Molins' original text had been published in 1987. For the preface of the 2007 edition he restated his principal contention, namely that in spite of the atrocities allowed by the Code Noir, not a single philosopher of the Enlightenment rose to denounce it. Montesquieu, Voltaire, Rousseau thought and wrote about laws, history, philosophy, the human condition as if they did not know about the Code Noir and, if they knew, they chose to treat it and the subject matter as irrelevant. For example, when Rousseau wrote about slavery, he clearly never had in mind the one that Louis XIV had legislated by issuing, in 1685, the Code Noir.[12]

As stated earlier, the crucial issue facing the philosophers of the Enlightenment, and their intellectual inheritors today, is whether or not Africans count equally on the scale of humanity. Slaves still exist, but out of Atlantic slavery, an unacknowledged crime against humanity, something worse than slavery grew: the steady reinforcement of a mindset rooted in the idea that from the

power and wealth accumulated through it, impunity for the criminals is the rule while they can, through the International Criminal
Court, for example, prosecute, judge and sentence whomever
they choose to be the black sheep of what they consider the international community. The forms of enslavement have changed, but
the power relations between those who control wealth and the
poor remain as difficult to challenge as when slaves confronted
the slave owners.[13] The logic of the slave-owning class, over the
years and centuries, has been reproduced and reinforced as their
wealth continues to be generated through unfettered control over
the lives of hundreds of million of people.[14] Indeed, control has
become more and more anonymous, removing, or so it seems,
responsibility from the decision makers and leaving it in the
hands of the market. The inheritors of the slave owners could
almost claim that the market has democratised relations between
the owners of wealth and those without whose labour there
would be no wealth. Ideologically, they go further: without them
(their initiative, intelligence, competitiveness, etc) the workers
would not exist. An echo from slaving days?

The importance of the misunderstanding or, perhaps, refusal
to understand how humanity went from crime to crime against
itself, cannot be overstated. Could it be that, like a thief who gets
away with a crime, there grew a sense that the only way to ensure
one was never caught was to always run ahead. Put in a different
way: from the times when one of the roots of capitalism nurtured
itself on a twin crime against humanity, it was bound to seek to
reproduce itself by seeking to cover its tracks as efficiently as it
could.[15]

Mending and healing between Gaza and Haiti: the Niger Delta[16]

There are so many Gazas, so many Haitis and so many in between,
historically and geographically, that our attention focuses only on
the latest outrage. Walls are not only built on the ground, but
also in our minds. They are proliferating not only in Palestine or
South Africa, but wherever the excess of wealth seeks to prevent
the victims from seeing the privileges the wealthiest lavish on
themselves.

11

If through the centuries there had been a living memory spot on earth (one which had recorded everything, like the black box of aeroplanes), what might best represent or illustrate the criminal nature and essence of capitalism in all of its various phases since Atlantic slavery? The Niger Delta would be a strong contender. Generations after generations, the inhabitants of the Niger Delta have lived through the horrors of trading humans, palm oil and now oil. The literature on each of these predatory phases is voluminous, but for connecting these phases in history and fiction, the following recent works could be a starting point: *Where Vultures Feast: Shell, Human Rights, and Oil*, by Ike Okonta and Oronto Douglas (Verso, 2003); *Curse of the Black Gold: 50 Years of Oil in the Niger Delta*, photographs by Ed Kashi, edited by Michael Watts (Powerhouse Books, 2008); *Half of a Yellow Sun*, by Chimamanda Ngozi Adichie (Knopf, 2006).

As the title of historian G. Ugo Nwokeji's essay[17]– 'Slave ships to oil tankers' – suggests things have not changed much structurally speaking: wealth is still being extracted at an extravagant rate and in horrendous ways. The Niger Delta could be compared to a mini Democratic Republic of Congo because it is suffering from a resource which is avidly sought by multinationals, but it could also be compared to Gaza: the Niger Delta being to Gaza what the Nigerian federal government is to Israel. The inhabitants of both places suffer the same kind of treatment: pauperisation, humiliation, military attacks against unarmed civilians, severe deterioration of the health and educational systems. As in Gaza, it is dangerous to live in the Niger Delta. Not simply because of the constant harassment from the Nigerian Army, but also from environmental conditions which might be considered unacceptable to human beings. The pictures by Ed Kashi in *Curse of the Black Gold* speak volumes, but, at the same time, it is as if even pictures cannot quite tell the story of what has happened to the members of humanity who live in the Niger Delta.

From the fictional story of Kaine Agary, 'My blessing, my curse',[18] one comes face to face with a reality, which is not just peculiar to the Niger Delta, when a son has no better solution to his own predicament than to help a gangster prey on his mother. And to the mother's bewildered question why the son is doing this to her (she is being killed), the son's reply seems improbable: 'Mama, I do this because I love you'.[19]

The mind boggles in the face of what can only be called an illustration of how human conscience is being desertified to the point of having lost the capacity to nurture something as fundamental as love.[20] In situations such as these, comparisons are not very helpful because there is no such a thing as a Richter scale of human suffering, but one should be able to nurture humanity's conscience as a way of ensuring that it does not become framed by the principle that might is right, always. Kaine Agary's story is emblematic of the state humanity has reached. Humanity has been degrading itself without being aware of it, but with determined help from the might-is-right corner. The process of losing its conscience is much more advanced than it is aware of. At the same time it has been losing its consciousness.[21]

How does humanity recover from this long tortuous and tortured descent into steady and increasing destruction of itself, of the life principle? Increasing calls are coming from those who rely on images of how life on the planet is being destroyed (e.g. Al Gore's *An Inconvenient Truth*, Yann Arthus-Bertrand's *Home*). Yet, these calls have been coming for years, centuries, from the very victims of that process: women, children, Amerindians, Arawaks, Indians, native North Americans, Africans, Pygmies, San of South Africa, desert nomads, Dalit, etc. The calls from all these groups never received the same attention as that given to those who now have the ear of the rich and the mighty.

The mighty are listening to nature because nature does not lie and nature is more powerful than the mighty and the rich, in the end. But the mighty and the rich still see themselves as the ones who know better than anyone how to fix what is wrong. However, this time around, as usual the rich and the mighty still think that they can buy time, but nature's clock, being blind and insensitive to corruption, continues ticking. Yann Arthus-Bertrand has reiterated in interviews that the only way out of the current environmental crisis is by scaling down growth and consumption. Some of his supporters, however, think that people should keep consuming more and more … 'differently'.[22]

The wounds are everywhere on the planet and all of its living inhabitants, animals, plants and humans, but the rich and the mighty only want to see the wounds on the environment, not on the humans, especially if they belong to places like Africa. Listening to nature speaking through the voices of those who were wounded, tortured, killed in the process of destroying a way of living is a humbling exercise which could lead to healing, as shown, for example, in *Bamako*, Abderrahmane Sissako's compelling movie.[23] For the rich and mighty to acknowledge that they have been wrong could be the beginning of real change in how humans relate to each other, to nature, to the past, to the present and to the future of humanity. The solution to the current crisis will not come from minds focused on technological, economic and/or financial solutions. It will come from a reordering of priority, and a radical transformation of the relationship between human beings, in solidarity away from charity.

Notes

1. Many thanks to Andrew Lichterman for having drawn my attention to 'Relocating energy in the social commons' by John Byrne, Cecilia Martinez and Colin Rugero which appeared in the *Bulletin of Science, Technology and Society*, vol. 29, no. 2, April 2009, http://ceep.udel.edu/publications/2009_pe_BSTS_relocating_emergy_social_commons_Byrne_Martinez_Ruggero.pdf, accessed 9 December 2009. The article is excellent at the level of diagnosis, but falls short at the level of prescriptions because it fails to point out the fact that while most western (and westernising) societies have let go of the practices related to the commons, other societies, especially those enslaved and colonised by the West, still maintain close connections and practices to commons and to nature. But the ruling cliques of the West, as was with abolition, are certainly not about to acknowledge that they were wrong. French sociologist Edgar Morin, in an opinion piece in *Le Monde* of 12 June 2009 follows the same tendency: 'Changer le rapport de l'homme à la nature n'est qu'un début'. Only the West understands best what is best for the rest of the world.

2. My thanks to E. Wamba dia Wamba for having introduced me to the work of Jacques Camatte and, in particular, his *Gloses*, where he suggests that humanity's future is much gloomier than most people are willing to admit. See http://www.aaargh.codoh.com/blog/revifr/, accessed 9 December 2009. Camatte's strongest contention against capitalism is that it will be unable (unwilling even) to resolve its own contradictions and, consequently, drag humanity toward self-destruction. The position taken in this essay is that humanity can either awake and heal, or continue toward the abyss.

3. Such a reading has been done by scholars, scientists and artists. One of the most outstanding, especially in his persistence, is the Ghanaian novelist Ayi Kwei Armah.

4. When spelled out by US leaders, security always implies the use of

military, economic and/or force to implement it. See John Perkins (2004) *Confessions of An Economic Hit Man*, San Fracisco, CA, Berrett-Koehler.

5. Noam Chomsky (2009) 'The torture memos and historical amnesia', *The Nation*, 19 May, http://www.thenation.com/doc/20090601/chomsky, accessed 8 December 2009.

6. Some of the essays pointing in this direction can be found in Robert S. Frey (ed) (2004) *The Genocidal Temptation: Auschwitz, Hiroshima, Rwanda and Beyond*, Lanham, MD, University Press of America. See also Darrell J. Fasching (1993) *The Ethical Challenge of Auschwitz and Hiroshima: Apocalypse or Utopia?* Albany, NY, State University of New York Press.

7. The importance of how this has been rationalised cannot be overemphasised as can be seen from Robert Jay Lifton's study on the concept of 'doubling' in *The Nazi Doctors: Medical Killing and the Psychology of Genocide*. Through 'doubling' ordinary people ended up rationalising how to do the most evil acts. The question is: during WWII, the doctors whose job it was to kill; could it be that 'doubling' has spread and affected those social scientists who today have been harnessed to push through the World Bank's structural adjustment programmes on so-called developing countries?

8. Pierre Nora, historian and intellectual, descendant of Marc Bloch, one of the founders of the Annales school of history in France, seems to have forgotten Bloch's warning contained in *Strange Defeat*, the book Bloch wrote, on the run, in order to understand why France had been invaded (defeated) without much of a fight at the beginning of WW II. After going through a laundry list of all those who were considered responsible for the defeat, Bloch concluded that the magnitude of the defeat was such that everyone was responsible.

9. This kind of denial is quite similar to the conviction that the Africans enslaved in Saint Domingue could not possibly think of freedom and, even if they did, they would not be able to pull it off. The difference between the past and the present is that everything is being done to ensure that 'mishaps' such as those that happened in Saint Domingue (or Cuba a century and a half later) do not happen again.

10. The reason for Ribbe's comparison has to do with locking up those who had surrendered into the vessels' holds and then burning sulphuric acid to asphyxiate them as the fastest way of killing them. Writing from Brazil, my reference is to the Portuguese translation (2008): *Os Crimes de Napoleão: Atrocidades que influenciaram Hitler*, Rio de Janeiro, Editora Record lda, especially pp. 146–51. See also Yves Bénot (1992) *La Démence coloniale sous Napoléon*, Paris.

11. Louis Sala-Molins (2007) *Le Code Noir ou le calvaire de Canaan*, Quadrige/ Presses Universitaires de France, p. x. Sala-Molins' comment is worth quoting in full: 'By charging the conscience tribunal of what belongs to the courts, through a somersault the legislator condemns for the benefit of the audience what it absolves through the law, abandoning to the ream of morality, where he has no business, what belongs to the law, where he

is sovereign. Let us not forget the strong words of Tocqueville at the time of the 1848 abolition of slavery: "If the blacks have a right to be free, it is unquestionable that the settlers have the right not to be ruined by the freedom of the blacks"' (Sala-Molins, 2007, p. 277, as cited from Tocqueville, *De l'émancipation des esclaves, OC*, t. 3, p. 105).

12. Sala-Molins (2007) pp. 237–54.

13. Just consider the difference of treatment between, say, bank executives and your average factory or office worker, or just plain citizen.

14. From such an angle, it is arguable that there are more 'enslaved' people today than during slavery.

15. This has been achieved in a way that the propaganda leaders of Hitler's regime could only dream of, thanks to the combined efforts of the advertising and leisure industries, on the one hand, and the industrialisation of secular, religious and cultural practices, on the other. Crucial to the victory was a refusal to look at the marketers of the system in the manner that Jesus did when he threw them out of the temple.

16. 'Mending' alludes to MEND, the Movement for the Emancipation of the Niger Delta. For an understanding of how MEND came about, see Michael Watts' 'Sweet and Sour', Dimieari Von Kemedi's 'Nero's Folly' and Tom O'Neill's interview 'Grand Commander' (the leader of MEND) all in Watts, Michael (ed), photographs by Ed Kashi (2008) *Curse of the Black Gold: 50 Years of Oil in the Niger Delta*, Brooklyn, NY, Powerhouse Books, pp. 36–47, 190–1 and 196–7.

17. Watts (2008) pp. 62–5.

18. Watts (2008) pp. 153–4.

19. Watts (2008) p. 153.

20. In Toni Morrison's novel *Beloved*, the fugitive (slave) mother who gives birth to a child while escaping from slavery decides to kill the child when slave hunters are about to recapture her because she cannot bear the idea of the child growing up under slavery. While that act can be seen as an act of love, the same cannot be said about the son helping the gangster's robbery and the slashing of his mother's throat. Nevertheless, in both cases, it illustrates the kinds of transformations which can, under extreme circumstances, alter the conscience of human beings.

21. Aside from the evidence already mentioned above, the signs of how this process is unfolding can also be found in the works of Nicholas Carr, for example in 'Is Google making us stupid?', http://www.theatlantic.com/doc/200807/google, accessed 9 December 2009.

22. http://www.lemonde.fr/planete/article/2009/06/03/arthus-bertrand-l-image-de-marque_1201679_3244.html#ens_id=1201789, accessed 9 December 2009.

23. Among film directors, Abderrahmane Sissako has captured very well the moment in which we are living. At the end of a discussion of his movie *Life on Earth* (1998), he states his vision of the kind of world he would like to see by pointing out how dangerous the world has become. In a world in which money has become virtual, the same world could self-destruct 'virtually'. See

http://video.google.com/videoplay?docid=-6311553641487110218, accessed 9 December 2009. In other words, whereas weapons used to be central to physical destruction, extreme financial engineering today makes possible a real destruction of the world through virtual economic and financial speculation. In this kind of world, the most powerful nation can actually become the weakest.

2

In solidarity with Cité Soleil/ Site Soley in Haiti

22 March 2007

In the age of globalisation why do we not see, on a world scale, cases of twinning in solidarity with cities such as Cité Soleil in Haiti; Abahlali in Durban, South Africa; Ndjili in Kinshasa, DRC? All are places, like *favelas* the world over, brimming with youth and creativity, but confronted with easily eradicable unhealthy conditions of living.

Why, given its namesake, does Sun City in South Africa not come out in solidarity with the poorest of the poorest in the allegedly poorest country of the western hemisphere? It may sound childishly naïve, but would not such a move be immanently expected from a city in the country that got rid of apartheid thanks, in part, to the selfless work of millions around the world?

From the inhabitants of all these places, there seems to only be one call that could, should bring us all together: Fidelity to Haiti, 1804. Thought through, away from nation state ideologies, away and against the corporate models of accumulation, such a call has the potential for healing humanity, taking it to the level many dreamed of while battling apartheid in South Africa.

Sun City in South Africa is known as the capital of gambling, where fortunes are spent in hopes of making even bigger fortunes. To those who would rather visit Sun City in South Africa than Cité Soleil in Port-Au-Prince, poverty is something to run away from, not something to embrace, even if these same people will make sure that their admiration for the one who epitomised poverty – Francis of Assisi – is well advertised. Should not such ongoing contradictions lead one to ask why more and more people are getting poorer and poorer, while a few accumulate wealth?

Since the end of apartheid, South Africa now boasts black billionaires, just like other African countries. Is it not possible to ask what would happen if the mindset which drives gambling turned instead to eradicating the differences between the Cités Soleil and Sun City?

Cité Soleil means Sun City in French, and that is where President Jean-Bertrand Aristide trained himself, beyond the reach of the mindset of the Haitian elite and beyond the bureaucratised seminarian teachings of love, which sterilise as they happen.

But it was through such tight embracing solidarity with the poor people of Haiti, and not just those of Cité Soleil, that President Aristide broke the comforting and comfortable chains of charity. This is also why politician theoreticians, theologians and ideologues of all stripes, and from opposite corners, do not – or pretend not to – know where he belongs. Why, one hears them thinking, does he side with losers?

Of the admirers of Francis of Assisi we may ask: if your idol were to come back to earth, say in Haiti, where would he most likely go to ask for hospitality? Isn't condemning poverty from the confines of billions in wealth and property the surest way of intensifying poverty and increasing the ranks of the poor? Canonised, Francis must be good to have on one's side.

The mindset among the owners of capital which led them to treat human beings as a means of further accumulation is still as entrenched as ever: capital reigns supreme, not only through its own corporate structures, but also through subservient nation states which have become so submissive that they willingly dissolve themselves in front of it; and not just in the countries where the structural adjustment programmes of the World Bank and the IMF were pioneered, such as in Mobutu's Zaïre.

Although invented by the military for military purposes, low intensity warfare against the poor can best be conducted using economic, financial and real weapons, especially if, as is the case in Cité Soleil, it is done through hired soldiers from such places as Sri Lanka, Brazil, Jordan and Nigeria. Black on black violence has always been easier to defend and ignore ideologically than the white on black kind, especially in Haiti.

From Haiti to South Africa: 1804–1994–2004

For 13 years, 1791 to 1804, people from various parts of Africa – about 500,000 people, half of whom had been born in Africa – decided that slavery was inhuman. Rather than live under it, they decided it was better to fight it – to death, if necessary, without generals trained in military academies, without outside help of any kind. The Wretched of the Earth gave a 13 year-long lesson in organisation, discipline and solidarity in order to bring about equality, fraternity and liberty. They did so without the help of human rights. Indeed, as will be argued below, this massive and successful trespassing played a crucial role in triggering human rightism as we know it today, a charitable way of helping, while preventing the kind of solidarity called for by the revolutionary slogan 'equality, fraternity and liberty'.

The slaves went further than the enlightenment philosophers ever thought possible. They went further then the leaders of the French Revolution were prepared to go in 1789. It was not until 1792–94, during the period of the Convention (known as the Terror) that slavery was finally abolished. The slaves had done the improbable, the impossible, the forbidden. In short, they had surpassed themselves and, in the process, they also trespassed.

The overthrow of slavery is still difficult to comprehend today. It does not fit easily into the ideological narratives of the left or the right. Aside from CLR James' *The Black Jacobins*, that feat was so exceptional, given the times and probability of success, that it has not received the attention it deserved from historians, philosophers, theoreticians. At the same time, it receives persistent negative attention from the powers that be in the form of imposed debt repayments (so-called compensation for the slave and plantation owners), invasions, occupations, international kidnapping of an elected president, prison, torture, and collective punishment of people from all walks of life whose only crime was fidelity to 1804.

With President Jean-Bertrand Aristide currently in involuntary exile in South Africa, it is difficult not to examine the relationship between anti-slavery and anti-apartheid, two battles which unfolded at different times, under different conditions, both with the common objective of seeking freedom.

Given the quasi house arrest under which Aristide is held in South Africa, is it unreasonable to ask oneself how the South African political leadership sees its role in the battle to bring Haiti to where it should have been, in the first place, since 1804? Could it be that Mbeki sees his role as reasoning with Aristide to accommodate himself to the demands of those who are in charge of the world today? The question may sound unfair and unreasonable. But is it? After all, Mbeki was the lone African head of state at the 200th independence anniversary in January 2004. The entire South African white-owned press was rabidly against it.

Too many questions which should be raised are not being raised. Why such a deafening silence only after President Aristide was given asylum in South Africa? Could it be that the two centuries of punishment which have been inflicted on Haiti have dampened the enthusiasm of those who might be tempted to stand by in solidarity?

Final question, how can any country, let alone an African one, lend its services to a process which included the kidnapping of a democratically elected president? It bears striking similarity to what happened more than 200 years ago when Toussaint L'Ouverture, the leader of the Haitian Revolution, was taken prisoner by the country which is known in history for its 1789 Revolution. By then, in 1802, everything was being done to quash what the Africans had done. Could it be that the leadership of South Africa has become so subservient to the powers that be (US, France, Canada, the Vatican) as to allow itself to be seen as a willing participant in an operation more reminiscent of the times when Steve Biko was arrested?

From our collective histories, we might look at the role being performed by the South African leadership as similar to the one performed by Tshombe in Katanga, when the West needed to get rid of Lumumba.

From trespassing to punishment (1825–1938/46)

With the rise of Napoleon, the process of collective punishment was initiated. Military attempts to reverse the victory of the Africans in Haiti failed. The Africans were able to repel the three best armies of the day: French, Spanish and English. By 1825 however, the Haitian government was forced by France, with the help of the US, Canada and the Vatican, to agree to pay compensation to the slave and plantation owners, in exchange for being accepted as a nation state. Repayments for the liberty of the former slaves were made until 1938, according to some, to 1946, according to others. Having lost militarily and politically, the former slave owners sought to reassert their authority in the international arena, where their control was unchallengeable.

From the viewpoint of the former slave and plantation owners, they had to show that emancipation by the slaves, in their own terms, could not be acceptable, regardless of whether those terms (emancipation) replicated ideological tenets held by the slave and plantation masters.

The collective and severe punishment which followed 1804 is in line with the syndrome of discovery, which can be stated as follows: discoverers shall always be discoverers, and should discovered ones discover anything, especially something universally acceptable such as emancipation, they shall be put back in their place.

In the case of the slaves overthrowing slavery in Haiti, the virulent vengeance of the response has not abated, two centuries after the event. Indeed, the arsenal has grown bigger, multi-headed, more sophisticated.

Opponents of the eradication of slavery are still being corralled by the United States which has seen itself as guardian of the treasures and resources accumulated by and through their discoveries: USA, France, Canada, the Vatican – and they are not the only ones. The resort to the political and financial punitive measures mentioned above, combined with secular and religious ideological orthodoxies, were meant to divide the Haitian people.

As it has been observed in many post-colonial situations, a small privileged elite saw itself as the only worthy Haitians. The syndrome of discovery has remained as virulent as ever: slaves must not free themselves; the poor must not end poverty on their own terms. The poor of Cité Soleil, by definition, according to the elite, must not have a voice, except as filtered or reframed by the media controlled by the elite.

From full rights to human rights

The slaves wanted to be treated as full human beings with the same full rights available to the masters. In their battle, there was no plan B, no halfway to freedom. From the 1804 event, those who continue to suffer from injustices, structural and circumstantial, have been told the same message, over and over: only the discoverers can discover the solutions to injustices. Whereas the slaves battled for full rights, their descendants in Haiti and all over the planet are being told that their way out of oppression and exploitation can only take place through the charitable detours of human rights. The average person in the world can see for herself that the 1804 event has been followed by institutionalising processes aimed at sterilising all the possible consequences which could, and should, have led to more and more emancipation from the shackles born out of the capital accumulated through slavery, land theft in North America and colonial occupation.

Despite the pious mantras coming out of political, religious and financial centres of power, the majority of humanity continues to be enslaved by a dominant economic system which thrives on poverty. When US defence secretary McNamara left the Pentagon for the World Bank after the Vietnam debacle, he vowed to end poverty within a decade.

Having lost, the slave masters, the plantation owners and their allies did everything to ensure that the process of change should never be set by those who had suffered and been dehumanised the most. In the case of Haiti, Napoleon Bonaparte sent his best troops to reinstate slavery, and the mindset of political theorists like Tocqueville remained resolutely unchanged when it came to slavery, pointing out, among other things, that 'France …does not want to destroy slavery and then suffer the pain of seeing the bankrupted whites leaving the colonies and [seeing] the blacks falling back into barbarism.'[1]

The 100 plus years of repayments were about denying the Haitians the ability to invest in their future. And so it has been since: in the US, the abolition of slavery went hand in hand with measures aimed at ensuring that former slaves did not think they could just walk away from their masters. Angela Davis, in *Are Prisons Obsolete?*, highlighted what other writers before her had noticed: abolition gave way to the introduction of legislation aimed at keeping the former slaves in check, leading seamlessly to what has become known as the prison-industrial complex. In the south, the majority of the prison population turned, almost overnight, from white to black. It took a century for the former slaves to get the right to vote, but this voting has come with all kinds of institutionalised limits.

During the colonial period in the DRC, the end of colonial rule could only be envisioned as a series of half measures. The colonial subjects were forced or indoctrinated to think of themselves through the legal, administrative, social and political prism of the subjugators. By now it should be clear: there must always be a sharp and unbridgeable gap between the rich and the poor, as there had to be between the coloniser and the colonised. Visible and non-visible 'no trespassing' signs are everywhere with the result that the poor keep getting poorer and the rich, richer.

From Kongo to Haiti to DRC-Congo: 1706–1757–2007

The way world history has been written by the victors had one prerequisite: make sure that the vanquished have no doubt about their vanquished status. It is not just that given episodes have different names (e.g. enlightenment, civilisation, Cold War, development, globalisation). It is above all the erasure of the mindset of those who, against all odds, refused to submit to dehumanisation, not just in their own name, but in the name of the larger community, including those who were dehumanising them.

If the French government has finally passed a law acknowledging that slavery had been a crime against humanity, why then, have those who did fight it not been acknowledged as heroes, heroines, saints? Not just in France, but also in their own countries? Why hasn't Kimpa Vita (Dona Beatrix), burnt at the stake for denouncing the Kingdom of the Kongo's king for allowing the slave trade and slavery to continue, not been considered for sainthood by the hierarchy of the Catholic Church? What prevents the current Congolese government from acclaiming her and explaining in detail why she is a national heroine?

In 1757, in Haiti, a man known as Makandal was caught and burned at the stake in 1758 because he had been accused of having killed, by poisoning, many slave owners. A generation later, in 1791, another slave, Boukman, played a crucial role in the ritual which is considered as the start of the uprising which led to the 1804 victory. These are the well-known names, but over and above them, millions of anonymous people battled dehumanisation, often falling into dehumanising violence, but holding on to the conviction that slavery was a crime against life, against humanity. Why do we not see schools, hospitals and research institutes, from Mozambique, around the Cape to Senegal bearing the above names, as a way of reintroducing the way they thought and fought into our collective consciousness?

Haitian elites, generally, with a few exceptions, have ended up siding with the descendants of the slave owners, and it is these elites who worked hard to comply with the repayments. Theoretically, Aristide was a bona fide promising member of the elite, but he veered away from the elite and the Catholic Church hierarchy to follow a course reminiscent of that of Reverend Beyers Naude in South Africa, when he refused to go along with the Dutch Reformed Church's support of apartheid. The virulence with which some members of the Haitian elite have attacked Aristide makes one wonder whether it is less of a crime to discriminate against the poor in Haiti than to discriminate against the blacks in South Africa.

From Toussaint L'Ouverture to Lumumba to Machel

These three leaders are national heroes in their own countries. At the same time, it is not difficult to see that the current elites in those countries would rather maintain some distance from them. In all three cases, there has been reluctance on the part of those states responsible for their death to go beyond formal apology.

In the case of France and Toussaint, Louis Sala-Molins suggested that full recognition of responsibility and apology, say during the 1989 bicentenary of the French Revolution, could have been followed with placing Toussaint's remains next to Napoleon's sarcophagus in the Pantheon in Paris. Later on, the French state gave itself another opportunity to do exactly that by proclaiming slavery a crime against humanity. We are still waiting.

Following Ludo de Witte's book *The Assassination of Lumumba*, coming after Adam Hochshild's *King Leopold's Ghost*, the Belgian state showed the same kind of cowardice. Again, it is not difficult to suspect the reasons: fear that people would seek revenge. This is the same mindset which prevented white South Africans from opening up for a long time: if they – the blacks – win, they will throw us into the sea. But, at the same time, just as in Haiti, a black South African elite has emerged which finds itself closer to those who have always vilified the likes of L'Ouverture, Lumumba or Machel. All the while, of course, singing the praises of Nelson Mandela.

The case of Samora Machel is the most interesting because it is the most recent. His figure is in the process of being erased from the historical conscience of Mozambique. Machel died in a plane crash on 19 October 1986, but the 20th anniversary of his death was a low-key celebration. And the reason why is obvious: 20 years after his death, things are going on in Mozambique which would have been unacceptable to Samora Machel.

An open letter to the world's citizens

Dear friends,

203 years since the slaves of Saint Domingue overthrew slavery, against the most formidable armies of the day, humanity, not just the descendants of slaves, should be celebrating that event. But instead of celebration, one sees almost the exact opposite. UN troops in Haiti are carrying out regular killings of babies, women and old people in one of the poorest neighbourhoods of Port-Au-Prince, Cité Soleil. We should do better than just stand by, shaking our heads, occasionally protesting. Should we not change gear in our daily lives and vow not to stop till Haiti is completely free as it was meant to be in 1804?

Instead of outraged solidarity, there is a massive silence, aside from a few solitary voices expressing solidarity in various cities around the world. Sadly, some of the best-known anti-apartheid leaders, in and outside South Africa, have been ingenious at explaining the apathy which really boils down to refusing solidarity with the inhabitants of a small island.

Why? One well-known and courageous anti-apartheid leader

(non-South African) went for the generic, easy comment: 'until Haiti has an ANC type party which could be supported, it is not worth doing anything'.

Then there have been the vicious attacks against Jean-Bertrand Aristide by members of the Haitian elite, who had no shame in publishing a letter in the white-owned press of South Africa, saying that Aristide is no Mandela. Well, thank God for that. Even Mandela himself would hope that there are others from the continent and beyond to carry on from the point reached in the battle against South African apartheid.

When looking in the rear mirror of history, from the surrounding extremes of wealth and poverty, of stupendous spending on weapons systems as against caring for people, it is easy to ask oneself: whether slavery, or more precisely, the mindset unleashed by the system, was ever abolished? More and more, it appears that slavery was simply modernised to get rid of the aspects standing in the way of cheapening labour.

With Auschwitz and Hiroshima/Nagasaki, it is not just labour which became cheaper. Life lost its sacredness and became dispensable on a massive scale, leading Einstein to say, right after Hiroshima/Nagasaki, that with the splitting of the atom, everything changed completely – except the way we think. Surely, my friends, it is high time to change the way we think if we are going to move on from that mindset. The same preoccupation could be expressed differently: 'When did thinking as humans begin to disappear?'

Who defines terror?

From the viewpoint of the discoverers, terror is only terror when it terrorises them, their descendants or their friends. Never, or so it seems, are they willing to imagine the terror which was experienced by the anonymous couple who, on any day in the 18th century, somewhere on one of those slave routes to the Atlantic, were kidnapped by armed mercenaries coming out of nowhere in the middle of the night, who dragged them away, screaming and crying.

Their terror can only be comparable to what would happen later during the Second World War, in Europe, when people would be dragged out of their houses to be put on cattle trains and sent to an unknown destination. The Africans were taken like cattle to waiting ships, packed like sardines. How would one document the terror they felt? Through their numbers, costs, bills of lading? Conceivably and imaginatively, the only archives where their terror could be found would be in the archives lying at the bottom of the Atlantic, and retrievable only through specially conducted healing ceremonies. Such terror, if it could be brought back to life for healing purposes, might help the monopolisers of terror and violence see for themselves the roots where it all begun.

Retaliating against terror with more terror can only mean the triumph of the terrorising mindset, of terror as the best possible weapon. Fighting terror with terror is another way of taking us back to the mindset of the Cold War, which is but a continuation of the mindset which underlay slavery. It is a mindset which leads to death, not to life.

The anonymous couple were quickly separated: women on one side and men on another. Their peaceful lives had been violated, but what was to follow was beyond anything they thought human beings could inflict on others. Soon, their separation would be completed when she found herself on one ship; he, on another. Still, like any human being, she began to look on the positive side of things: she was still alive, in relatively good health, and, with a new life inside her womb, she had with her a bit of her husband: her duty was to protect this new life to the best of her ability. Being at peace in a context of violence is one of the most stressful tasks ever.

To summarise, it suffices to say that the ship's captain had spotted her among the others, and told the sailors to prepare her as one of his travel companions. The question is, how and who will ever tell the story of how she was raped repeatedly. How she eventually decided to take her life by throwing herself off the ship.

More to the point, where and how is it possible to heal such massive, individual and collective, indescribable wounds whose effects are still rippling across these people's descendants centuries later?

Who defines poverty?

Haiti, 'the poorest country of the so-called "western" hemisphere' reads the lamentation billboards of the western media. As if Haiti and its poverty is a stain on the image expected to be projected by the West, or a tortuous warning to those who might be interested in following the same route: you will be crushed so badly that no one else will be tempted to think beyond the path traced by the discoverers and abolitionists.

The so-called poor of Cité Soleil do not see themselves as the poor framed by the crocodile tears shed by humanitarianists. The triumph of the slaves in 1804 happened because they did not dwell on being slaves; and so it is with the poor. The poor see themselves as being endowed with the capacity to overthrow the mindsets which keep insisting that they, the poor, can only be helped out of poverty by charitable gestures and structures.

Overthrowing poverty, like overthrowing slavery, can only be tackled, and succeed, as a political gesture. But because everything has been done and continues to be done by those who did not want the slaves to succeed, the battle over slavery, and its history, continues to this day. It extended into colonial rule, with the same message: do not ever trespass over the boundaries of power. If you do, expect the worse kind of punishment.

From 1804 to this day, the history of Haiti continues to unfold along two distinct paths: the one left by Toussaint and those who did overthrow the system; and the one which the slave owners, plantation owners and their allies could never ever let go, at the risk of losing more than their own possessions.

With globalisation, the stakes have not changed: on the one hand, there are those who state that the slaves were wrong. They did not know what to do with what they achieved, economically, politically. They inherited the economic jewel of the French colonial possessions, and 'ruined' it. Those who had lost that battle in Saint Domingue resorted to their allies to impose conditions on the new state, which ensured that whatever economic gains the former slaves made would be siphoned off to those who had insisted on compensation.

In today's world where everyone is being called on to globalise, or else in the wake of a system which has relentlessly modernised itself since the days of industrialised Atlantic slavery, should we not be proud to have amongst us people who are saying no to such a call? In these times of addiction to wealth seeking, is it not admirable to have people, known and unknown, who are refusing to be seduced by the promises of a system, the annihilating capacity of which, physical and spiritual, has reached incommensurable proportions?

We face today the same odds that the slaves in Haiti faced against the system, then in its infancy. Is it not true that we keep hearing that the only way to improve the lot of humanity is to forget our humanity in order to save ourselves later, by following the very mindset which has brought us to such a precarious point? Is it not true that, individually and collectively, we are being asked to stop exercising our capacity to think? Is it not true that we are being trained to look with fear and mistrust at some of our best, non-violent life instincts?

The process of destroying humanity over the last 500 years never stopped. Now and then, it has slowed down, but on the whole, from trespassing on life to trespassing on the living, the system which emerged out of glorifying itself by attrition, against existing damning evidence, has now reached an unprecedented level of domination. By pretending that one suffering was worse than another, by pretending that comparing suffering was insulting to those who considered themselves the worse sufferers, that which was indivisible was cut to pieces.

From Hispaniola to Hiroshima, the splitting mindset did not just attack the atom. Long before the physicists got their turn, the process had proceeded, practically unopposed, against so-called savages and barbarians, with occasional defenders. The native Americans' land was taken away from them, and with it, a way of thinking diametrically opposed to splitting the atom. From Hispaniola to Saint Domingue, the Arawaks were wiped out and replaced with people stolen, hijacked, terrorised away from their homes, their land, their fields in Africa. And yet, in Saint Domingue, the spirit of refusing to be split from humanity rose again, and against all the odds, triumphed, briefly, before revenge and collective punishment started again.

Who is the enemy?

The arsenal in place to eradicate humanity is visible everywhere: the armament industry could wipe out life on the planet and the planet itself several times over. Yet still, it keeps growing and being modernised. Have we not heard the argument before: if we shut down this or that factory, we would be taking jobs away from working people? But is it right to have a mindset which is always looking for enemies, even though such enemies only exist in the mindset of warmongers seeking to make sure that their products will always have buyers?

Do we not live in a world dominated by advertising and entertainment industries living off the by-products of warfare? It has been shown that war fought with weapons has become obsolete, that it is possible to annihilate your enemy by just manipulating the market. Has the triumphant mindset, such as it is, left only one exit for those looking for freedom? Have we not realised that this exit, framed by such a lethal mindset, will take us to a variation of something we have already seen, but this time it will be worse? Could it be that little by little, by attrition, humanity has completely given itself, its capacity to think and its sense of balance between the spiritual and the material over to the market?

Is there really any interest in wiping out poverty?

It is not difficult to see that the poor are the potential enemies of the global system, as run by the corporations and their crumbling nation state allies. A social, political and economic system which has prospered on the basis of dividing, discriminating to death and thriving on competition is wired to reproduce competition and discrimination. There will be conventions against poverty, just as there have been conventions against genocide. Charitable structures will be used to spread some of the dispensable, tax reducing profits. The system's growth has thrived on generating poverty. But, ideologically speaking, it must present itself as wanting to do something about poverty.

The abolitionist mode did not work with slavery. There is no reason why it would work in abolishing poverty, unless anchored in building greater social solidarity between all members of humanity. In short, fidelity to humanity as affirmed at turning points such as in 1804 in Haiti would be the serious way to get rid of poverty. Such fidelity will not happen overnight, but can grow out of healing processes initiated away from corporations and states, between members of humanity.

Note

1. Tocqueville (1987 and 2007) *De l'émancipation des esclaves, Oeuvre Complète,* t. 3, p. 105, as cited by Louis Sala-Molins, *Le Code Noir ou le calvaire de Canaan,* Paris, Presses Universitaires de France/Quadrige, p. 277.

3

The routes and possibilities of a South-South subversive globalisation: Africa and Brazil[1]

11 December 2007

Almost everyone knows about Brazilian football, especially Pelé, but it is a fair bet that only a tiny percentage of the same people will know about one of the foremost intellectuals of Brazil in the 20th century: Milton Santos, winner in 1994 of the Vautrin Lud prize given to the most outstanding geographer (sometimes known as the Nobel prize for geography). Others have described Milton Santos (1925–2001) as the Noam Chomsky of Brazil. One could go on with the accolades. Thanks to a recent documentary (directed by Silvio Tendler) about his ideas, Santos' reputation is likely to gain greater recognition among Brazilians as they begin to realise how far ahead was his visionary understanding of humanity's plight and challenges.

This is not an essay on Milton Santos; it is an encouragement to those who already know him, or of him, and those who do not, to get to know him better. It is also an appeal to those who have the wherewithal to contact the film-maker and make it available in other languages, including Kiswahili since Santos taught in the geography department of the University of Dar es Salaam in the mid-1970s.

The main purpose of this essay is to reflect on the growing convergence (economic, political and cultural) between Brazil and the Africa which is not delimited by its geographical borders. To paraphrase Milton Santos' view: surely, another kind of globalisation is not only possible, but a must if humanity is to be born.[2] Inexorably, it will be thought of and led by the poor, or the Wretched of the Earth, as Franz Fanon long ago saw coming. Will African intellectuals join them or prefer to continue mimicking the West?

33

Mimicking or thinking? 1804 or 184?

In one of his interviews (and in the documentary), Milton Santos lamented the fact that most Brazilian intellectuals were more interested in copying what is happening in Europe or in the USA, rather than thinking about where they are, where they have come from and where they would like to go. Calling it intellectual laziness, he pointed out that it is easier for people to consume than to produce. Obviously, he is not the first to have said this.[3] The question, however, for all thinking Africans as we enter the era of the 50th anniversaries of independence is: What happened after independence? Is it something one could reasonably describe as an event,[4] one which could or should have mobilised fidelity to what it meant? Were they events on the same scale as other previous emancipatory events, such as Quilombo de Palmares in Brazil (1597–1695), Haiti (1791–1804) and many other unknown feats of resistance? Which kind of subject emerged out of such a collective birthing event? Did independences rupture the colonising enterprise, like truths puncture lies? Did there emerge an emancipated subject in our individual and collective consciousness? Which kind of consciousness prevailed in our countries, 50 years after independence? We can point to heroes and heroines who did all they could to maintain fidelity to the emancipated subject which emerged out of that event. Each reader can fill in the dots.

In Haiti today, 184 is the number of people and institutions who signed a petition against President Aristide, denouncing him in a manner reminiscent of the Congolese who colluded with external forces to eliminate Patrice Lumumba back in 1960/1. Could 184 coincidentally be an apt metaphor of what happened to 1804,[5] the shrinking and squeezing of freedom, equality and fraternity to the point of a group of 184 wishing it never happened? Could it be said that the same process has occurred in many African countries, namely the reducing of independence not to an event, but to a transition used and abused by a small group to enrich themselves while the largest part of the population remained poor or got poorer? Shouldn't what happens to every single Haitian today, because of that transition from 1804 to 184, be of concern to all thinking human beings?

On 12 December 2007 it will be four months since the disappearance of Lovinsky Pierre-Antoine.[6] Kidnapping (or rendition?) might be a more appropriate word. How many (among those who knew of it) have made even a symbolic gesture, calling on his kidnappers to let him free? Kidnapping used to be one of the ways people were ripped from the continent and dragged to the forts and slave ships. Wherever he is, Lovinsky could be asking himself why there have not been greater efforts to get him back from where he is. He must wonder, like many others, why the Brazilian government, headed by a president who visited Gorée and, more or less,[7] apologised for slavery, does not go out of its way to go and find Lovinsky. Or, as some have speculated, is it part of the agenda of the UN mission in Haiti (MINUSTAH) to silence, completely, all those who have vowed to continue calling for the return of President Aristide to Haiti?

It is impossible to think of Africa 50 years ago without at the same time thinking about its history from 500 years ago, because it is only by looking over the entire period that one can begin to guess at the magnitude of the crime which has been committed with unimaginable, relentless impunity. If the Brazilian government, through its president, really meant to apologise for slavery, should it not be seen thinking and acting in a manner which is aimed at restoring the Haiti of 1804 rather than allying itself with the 184?

Brazil–Africa: South–South or South–North–South?

As more and more thinking Africans clamour for greater and greater South–South cooperation, it is encouraging to observe how the Brazilian government is willing to tread where its ruling clique would not like to go. The ruling clique is only interested in so-called realpolitik, and not in building a planetary future through healing emancipatory processes, even if, as everyone can see from the climatic changes, such a course is the only viable one. The ruling clique is more interested in fitting into the world as it is, rather than trying to build a different world in which solidarity with Africa (and Asia) would loom large. But the world as it is, as seen from G8 meetings and places like Davos, is not interested in solidarity with Africa;[8] Africa and all of the poor of the world – they tell us – will be rescued by charity.[9] The charitable option is the most logical given that even the G8 and Davos have lost their grip on world decision-making processes as these have been eroded by the weight and impact of financial decision centres via 'the markets'. Described as self-regulatory, these financial monsters are showing increasing signs of being out of control. How could it be otherwise, given that the few regulatory leashes in place have been removed so that these financial monsters could – so the logic went – even better self-regulate themselves.[10]

The pressure for greater solidarity with Africa, in Brazil, comes from its population of African ancestry and their allies (indigenous, landless, working, jobless people). Even the ruling clique cannot completely ignore the fact that more and more people in Brazil are clamouring for greater justice, and so occasionally, it has to be seen as responding to these demands. As an emerging country, Brazil wants to have a permanent seat at the UN Security Council. This is one of the objectives which has driven President Lula's foreign visits, including the visits to Africa and his recent stop in Burkina Faso.

As many readers of Pambazuka News know, 15 October 2007 was the 20th anniversary of Thomas Sankara's assassination, while president of Burkina Faso, along with 12 of his comrades. One can only presume that the ruling clique decided that one additional vote in its quest of a permanent seat at the UN Security Council should be achieved by any means necessary and therefore accepted the Burkina Be invitation to 'celebrate the 20th anniversary of the Burkina Be revolution'. In the eyes of Sankara's foes such an accolade from Brazil would help bury Sankara one more time. Or for good.

However, this cynical collusion to treat African history like a serviceable walking mat does help illustrate the longer process of how the splitting apart of humanity has been carried out by the very people who apologise in one venue and do the exact opposite in another. Most academics are likely to condemn these colluders. And yet, again, should one not ask the same question raised about the 184 in Haiti? However inconvenient it might sound, is it not the case that, overall, in the 50 years since independence, African people have been betrayed by those who were supposed to be thinkers and who, on paper at least, always like to be seen as being on their side? Independence as a truth, as an event, has been treated like a mere happening, one which did not make intellectuals change their world view of the past, the present and the future. Yes, however uncomfortable it might make us, each one of us should ask: Did I do all that could/should have been done, and more, to turn that emancipatory event into a real transformation of the colonial situation? If one thinks one did, then the result should tell one that it was far from enough.

Now and then the daily routine of the last 50 years has been ruptured by someone like Thomas Sankara who did try to stay faithful to independence as an event. As Milton Santos might have said, Sankara's courage was to think. Thinking, in a context dominated by mimicking, submission, keeping quiet, is the most courageous act, suggested Milton Santos. Pushing further: are intellectuals in Africa, of Africa, from Africa, thinking? Over the past 50 years, have we become, more or less, like the 184 of Haiti? Faced with either catechising or thinking, which has been the easier road to follow? What happens when one of the so-called 'discovered' (e.g. Lumumba, Aristide) 'discovers' something the 'discoverer' does not want discovered? Ever since 1804, that question has been answered unilaterally in only one way, over and over, almost like a silent but persistent internal prescription: shrink that 1804 to 184, from the outside and from within.

Lumumba (1960), Sankara (1987) and Aristide (2004)

Certainly none of these three would have passed the catechist exam for mimicry. In the world of African spirits, one could imagine Sankara's spirits, from wherever they are circulating, letting us know how they understand the difference between mimicking and thinking, between a revolution and its fake. Listening attentively, one might be able to hear the following from Sankara's spirits:

Why and how is it, that starting with resistance to dehumanising practices, structures, mentalities, from the beginning of humanity, but especially since our independence, our leaders (not just in Burkina Faso) have colluded with their worst enemies to liquidate those who were trying to change course? More importantly, why not have an open dialogue so that our own voices could be heard, against those whose version of events is patently self-serving?

Right after they got rid of my comrades and I, they began to say that they were the real revolutionaries. I would not have minded if, indeed, they went on pursuing (reaching new heights) what we had started together, but, instead they started describing the revolution from the moment of my liquidation, as they went on liquidating many of the projects we had initiated. Those we had planned were archived, never to be heard of again. As singers have sung before why is it that we get rid so easily of those who struggle with the poorest of the poor, and in their place put the defenders of the richest of the rich?

From where I am, it is easy to meet with fellow victims of liquidation, including those who faced their fate after liquidating countless of their own people themselves. One with a very long name from somewhere at the centre of our continent told me, crying like a child, that he wished he could go back and bring back to life the leader whose punishment was so severe that they dissolved his body in an acid bath. These liquidisers or liquidationists, after coming here, were confronted with the real history of our continent, one which, given what happened, is impossible to measure even by the standards imposed by those who claim no one has ever suffered more than themselves. These spirits are in such pain for what they did that it is difficult not to sympathise with them.

Here is what one of them said (there is no point naming names, but he is one of the main characters in Ahmadou Kourouma's *Waiting for the Vote of the Animals*): 'I knew our situation was bad, but first I really believed the stories of the experts on development who kept repeating that sooner or later tickling [sic] down would get everybody laughing all the way to the bank (just like it happened to me), but then it kept getting worse, and it is only after coming down here underground that I could see (literally from below) how bad the suffering has been. I had seen some of it above ground, but from down here, I could not imagine how extreme the level of suffering has been.'

'It is only now,' continued this crying spirit, 'that I understood how terribly, and horribly wrong I was. Somehow I bought into the notion that our suffering is lightweight, so trivial, not worth talking about, let alone, complaining. No one, not even some of our best *griots*, has been able to convey, in words what really happened, the terror, the fear that was inflicted through those wars of hunting for slaves. Those who escaped the brutal fate, either by luck or choice (becoming part of the hunters, in exchange for a few cowries, alcohol, cloth and/or guns), and their descendants, did their best to ensure that their own role remained unknown. In short, what we are witnessing today, is a repeat of what has happened before: it is not the first time that our kin has colluded in and with self-liquidation.'

Again in the world of the African spirits, one would hear the spirits of Zumbi (the hero of the Quilombo de Palmares[11]) and the spirits of Sankara meeting and commenting on the systematic downsizing, downgrading of the history of the continent, leading the 184 from Haiti and from other places to the point where downgrading would coincide with denigration and, finally, simply denial. Zumbi would say to Sankara: 'You know, my spirits tried to talk to Lula about that choice and make him see that visiting on that day would be the equivalent of laughing at our own 20 November which has been chosen by the African brothers and sisters to commemorate the day I was killed in 1695.[12] But there was so much interference, there was no way he could have heard me. Of course, part of the problem is that he is trying to satisfy everybody.'

Not long ago, France under President Chirac passed a law calling slavery a crime against humanity, but in a world where the nation state has become one more instrument of the financial oligarchy, the mindset which emerged out of slavery has been reinforced rather than weakened. Every time it looked like someone was about to correct the history of the continent, they went the other way, as if the ruling principle is to keep laundering it until it becomes unrecognisable. With forces trying to negate what happened and others deforming it beyond recognition, is it surprising that 50th anniversaries or any attempt to recognise a truth, an event is turned into its opposite, like the ruling clique of Burkina Faso celebrating the assassination of Thomas Sankara as the birth of something they call a revolution.

Undoubtedly, some readers will take issue with the raising of these discomforting questions. Others might even condemn it as a disguised way of celebrating Afro-pessimism or useless self-flagellation. The vast majority of Africans will not even be able to access these words, and yet, it is this vast majority which has been robbed of what could have happened, had there been more thinking than mimicking within African intellectuality.

To carry on as the African brothers and sisters (by now ancestors) did in Haiti, from 1791 through 1804, without any help from outside, without human rights organisations cheering on the sides, took a kind of courage which is difficult to imagine today. Yet, one must nurture the courage to say, as Milton Santos did in the documentary, that there has been no humanity, so far; only now is it being built, little by little. Universalism has always been preached as coming from the Enlightenment. To which Milton Santos replicated: 'we, Brazilians, are not universal because we fail to be thoroughly (sufficiently) Brazilians'. The same could be said of Africans. The failure has been one of not keeping at it: trying and trying to be sufficiently (i.e. more and more) African.

Brazil and the 10.639/2003 Law

In a context dominated by hesitations and vacillations, those who have most benefited from the systematic laundering of African wealth/history would like to keep on laundering it after each new phase, even if it means reducing the entire planet to an unliveable place for all of its inhabitants. Those who have been cowered into submission still know that they were right to resist, but are running out of the courage of 1804. They do see the 184 waving at them to join their side, which, from a distance, does look like paradise on earth. Among them a half-despairing Congolese mutters: 'do not get fooled'. 'Back home', he continued, 'we had someone who also built a so-called paradise in the equatorial forest at a place called Gbadolite.[13] Nature has returned. He and his paradisiacal Zaïre are gone.'

On the other hand, thanks to the work of people battling to carry on the spirits of Zumbi in Brazil, a law was passed in 2003, calling for the teaching about Africa and about the history of people of African ancestry in elementary and secondary schools (note that pre-primary and tertiary/higher levels are not mentioned). As with its passing, the implementation of this law will depend on keeping alive the spirits of Zumbi, Sankara and so many other known and unknown truth discoverers. In and of itself the law will not change the mindset, but it is arguable that the mindset will change faster, provided that on the African side there is the courage to respond to law 10.639/2003. There is no point spelling out the possible multiplicity of responses because each individual, each collective can generate emancipatory thoughts/ responses aimed at transforming the current situation for the better for everyone.[14]

More than laws will be needed. No thoughts will be too small, no thoughts will be too big once total and complete emancipation from the remaining shackles of 1804 are turned into the single minded objective for humanity wherever people of African descent live, which is everywhere on the planet.

Notes

1. Following the overthrow of President Jean-Bertrand Aristide at the beginning of 2004, the United Nations, pressured by the US and France, passed resolution 1542 in the Security Council creating the Mission des Nations Unies pour la stabilisation de Haiti (Minustah) 'to restore order'. The mission began in June 2004. Having provided the largest military contingent, Brazil assumed the leadership of the mission. What should be born in mind is the changing political and diplomatic context in which many emerging countries, including Brazil, would like to increase their role in UN organs such as the Security Council.

2. For those interested in knowing more on Milton Santos (in Portuguese), see the following sites: http://www.nossosaopaulo.com.br/Reg_SP/Educacao/MiltonSantos.htm and http://www.teatrobrasileiro.com.br/entrevistas/stoklos-santos.htm. There is also an interview/conversation with Gilberto Gil (in English): http://old.gilbertogil.com.br/santos/eentre_0.htm.

3. The number of people one could list here is too long and diverse, but among those who come to mind are C.L.R. James, Frantz Fanon, Malcolm X, Amilcar Cabral, Amiri Baraka, Ayi Kwei Armah, Mongo Beti, Walter Rodney.

4. An event, from Alain Badiou's point of view is something out of the ordinary, something – a truth – which punctures existing knowledge with something new, something which did not previously exist, for example the French Revolution in relation to the Ancient Regime or the uprising in Saint Domingue giving birth to Haiti. The truth is not something which happens ready made, it is the result of a process (truth procedure). Such truth procedures are carried forward by and through fidelity. Event, truth and fidelity are interlinked.

5. For more information on 184, see: http://www.ijdh.org/articles/article_halfhourforhaiti_1-10-06.htm.

6. For more on Lovinsky's disappearance see the article by Roger Annis

on Znet (27 September 2007) http://www.zmag.org/content/showarticle. cfm?ItemID=13901.

7. There is no space here to discuss whether Lula's apology in Gorée was properly carried out. I do think that apology alone is not enough, given what happened.

8. Davos could be best described as the recycled Berlin of 1884–5, i.e. the place where the most powerful people of the planet meet to decide the future of its inhabitants. It could also be described as the kitchen cabinet of the UN.

9. The literature on how poisonous/ruinous charity can be is growing. See, among others, Michael Maren, Naomi Klein. However, as one reads these authors, many will have the feeling that what they are saying has been said before. The syndrome of discovery is still at work, whether the above authors like it or not: for the West it is hard to accept that it went wrong, but it is willing to accept it being said by those it can trust. Another way of saying this: a slave who fights for freedom cannot be trusted by those who profit from slavery until, from the latter's corner emerges abolitionists who will then be celebrated as the discoverers of slaves' freedom.

10. Any reader interested in verifying this assertion should read *The Wall Street Journal* or the *Financial Times* at least twice a week.

11. Quilombo de Palmares is located in the state of Alagoas. It (and the generic word Quilombo) came to symbolise the resistance of Africans to slavery. At one point its population was estimated to have reached more than 30,000. From the end of the 16th century to 1695, all efforts to subdue Quilombo de Palmares failed. Its last leader Zumbi is celebrated as a national hero on the anniversary of his death, 20 November 1695.

12. Analogies can be misleading, but 20 November is Black Consciousness Day in Brazil. Its equivalent in the US would be Martin Luther King Day.

13. Sometimes known as the village where President Mobutu was born, Gbadolite was transformed from a small village into the 'Versailles of the jungle', with an international airport where Concorde could land. When Mobutu was overthrown in 1997, the palaces and mansions were looted.

14. Will this law be properly advertised in all of the Brazilian diplomatic and cultural missions abroad, especially in the countries with African ancestry? It is through such publicity that Africans outside of Brazil will know of these efforts and so be in a position to think, in turn, of how to respond.

4

Erosion of freedom: from Haiti to South Africa

22 May 2008

This is a brief report from a visit to Durban, to see for myself places like Kennedy Road, Motala Heights, to meet with people like S'bu Zikode and Shamita Naidoo whose words continue to impact us in a way which is still generating new thinking. We were on our way to meet people who can be described as the staunchest defenders of the poor and, by extension, of humanity.

Driving with Pauline from Maputo to Durban reminded her of her native lands in the Caribbean: sugar plantations after sugar plantations. However, for her, that was the 50s. Now, this was 2008, in the province of Kwazulu-Natal, where Jacob Zuma, the newly elected President of the ANC, comes from. For those who do not know, it is worth remembering, in the name of always connecting the dots, that President Jean-Bertrand Aristide presented a thesis in linguistics at the University of South Africa (Unisa) comparing Isizulu and Creole. I am still reading the thesis, which can be found online and downloaded. It was presented in November 2006. I hope and pray that President Aristide does get invited/encouraged to visit the place from where so many Haitians originally came: DRC. We could then look forward to another comparative thesis on Kikongo and Creole and another step in the process of reconnecting those who should never ever have been separated from each other.

Thanks to Richard Pithouse we were able to meet a few among those who constitute the heart of Abahlali baseMjondolo (AbM – the South African shack dwellers' association that started in Durban), including Shamita Naidoo at Motala Heights and S'bu Zikode at Kennedy Road. Besides wanting to see the faces behind the names we had heard about, we wanted to understand

43

how people like S'bu Zikode and his companions had attracted such wrath from Durban City officialdom in general, and from Superintendent of Police Nayager, in particular. We wanted to understand how in the country where apartheid was defeated, some of its practices are still alive and well.

Here were people who, living among the poorest of the poor, were standing up and insisting on being treated with respect and dignity, as called for by the South African constitution, but who, strangely, were being charged, beaten up and arrested by the police as though they were criminals. How could a police force, under the political leadership of the ANC, behave in a way that is reminiscent of the apartheid police?

This question could be formulated differently and, maybe, more generically, in a region and in a world where such drastic turns are no longer the exception: How do good people or, more precisely, people who could have become heroes/heroines of goodness/love have taken a wrong turn somewhere. Some may not like the jump, but visiting places like AbM could help understand how a Mugabe in Zimbabwe became what he is today, that is turning against his own people. Is it that easy to lose one's moral compass?

In a world where governments are saying they want to wipe out all forms and degrees of poverty from extreme to mild, from endemic to periodic, one might be forgiven for thinking that the poor themselves would be the most important allies in such a project. Unfortunately, not so when one listens to AbM. Instead what one hears and what one sees leads one to a frightening conclusion: how something akin to ethnic cleansing emerges, against defenceless people. The average person might balk at such an assertion. After all, cleansing has been more easily associated with genocidal behaviour against another ethnic group. Some might find it offensive and out of line to suggest that an ANC government could be accused of ethnic cleansing against the poorest of its citizens. Is it not better to think of a most outrageous hypothesis so that those who are currently responsible for its probable outcome might pause, pull back and change course?

What would it take to stop the violence against the poorest of the poor (pop)?

One of the possible explanations for the extreme hatred shown by Superintendent of Police Nayager can easily be understood once one understands that the 2010 Soccer World Cup is to be held in South Africa. FIFA may not have stipulated that all efforts must be exerted to keep all and any signs of extreme poverty out of sight but the message comes through and RSA is doing everything to hide the offending communities away. It is not difficult to understand the reasoning behind this: people who come to be entertained by the soccer extravaganza must not be disturbed by the sight of shacks. Such a sight could lead to some of the visiting audience, not to speak of the performers themselves, asking about the appropriateness of spending such huge amounts of money when significant segments of the local citizenry do not have access to adequate housing and amenities such as water and electricity.

2010 being just around the corner, South African officialdom, at least some of them, are implementing the most radical option in keeping poverty/the poor out of sight. In the process, these poverty/ethnic cleansers have affirmed, in various and modulated ways, that the poor are not worth listening to, that their voices do not count.

In a country where the lethal combination of racism and competition has left a legacy of gross injustice, is it too late to suggest that those who were trampled upon should be listened to with the greatest care possible? Is it too late to suggest that while the Truth and Reconciliation Commission was a step in the right direction, it was bound to fall short of the task at hand? Is it too late to suggest that those who understand their profession as that of repressing, oppressing and beating up, should be retrained to listen, attentively and, wherever possible, with compassion to the poor? Surely it is not too late to suggest that as long as the poor are not free from the consequences of apartheid, no one is free. (That is why on Freedom Day, the people at Kennedy Road marched to remind the South African Nation that, for them, this was Unfreedom Day.)

It will be a while before I digest all of the words from S'bu Zikode and his companions, but there is a phrase I shall never forget: 'We do not want money'. This is the crux of the matter. In a world driven by the profit motive, competition, greed, selfishness, S'bu reminded those who would listen that they are not interested in what the self-appointed discoverers of poverty would like to eliminate via charitable gestures. They want to be treated with respect, justice and dignity. In those cases where the law is broken, e.g. trying to get food, water and/or electricity, they are saying to the government 'look at our situation. It is an unacceptable one to any self-respecting human being'. Is such a demand so outrageous that it has to be met with the unleashing of extreme violence? Is such a demand so unreasonable that it cannot even be listened to?

When so much still remained to be said, we asked S'bu Zikode what was the way out. 'Healing', he said. Needless to say, given Ota Benga's motto – for peace, healing and dignity[1] – a very long exchange followed. In a post-apartheid South Africa, in a South Africa where the Truth and Reconciliation Commission had raised such expectations and led to such disappointments, is it too late to listen to those who articulate the spirit of reconciliation with the conviction of a Mandela or a Tutu? People like Nayager, Sutcliffe, Govender and many others who share their understanding – misunderstanding, really – of the poor, surely are in deep need of healing because in their minds the poor are not worth anything.

Is it too late, in the name of humanity, to slow down the race to join in globalisation, the race to be part of the first world, with the collateral damage of maiming, torturing, killing those who are not strong enough to keep pace? It is our hope that the voices of S'bu, Shamita, and their growing supporters, such as Bishop Rubin Philipp, will re-energise, re-awaken the flagging spirits of those who had a different vision of post-apartheid South Africa, one which was more in line with the prescriptions being enunciated with such clarity from the *favelas* of South America and many other parts of the world. Those voices are refusing to accept the transition which has taken South Africans, poor and rich, from the end of apartheid in South Africa to global apartheid.

Seeing the citizens of Kennedy Road, of Motala Heights, reminded us of their brothers and sisters in Haiti, in Brazil, India, and cities all over the world whose only prescription is to be listened to with respect, and justice as human beings. As they keep repeating over and over: they do not want charity, they want solidarity. They do not want to be treated as a humanitarian issue, they want to be treated as human beings. To them we say thank you for being strong, thank you for reminding us of our common humanity, thank you for your courage and serenity.

Note

1. See www.otabenga.org

5

Fear of emancipatory history in the DRC: from Kimpa Vita to Lumumba, to the women of Panzi

6 November 2008

As events unfold in the DRC the usual questions are being asked: who is responsible for the current war within the war – which never really ended in 2003 – and its ensuing humanitarian crisis?

In the pages of one of the most respected dailies of Kinshasa (*Le Potentiel*) well-known philosophers have offered conflicting ways of looking at and analysing the conflict. Who is General Nkunda, and why has he said that this time around that he will not stop in Goma (threatening to go all the way to Kinshasa)? What is the Rwandan government up to, besides pretending, disingenuously, that it has nothing to do with it? Why is the Congolese army unable (or is it unwilling?) to defeat Nkunda's army? Does Nkunda take his orders from Kigali? Or from Kinshasa? Why has the AU remained so silent? Who is this current crisis going to benefit? Is this the prelude to the final and complete return of Mobutism without Mobutu? What is the UN (and its acolytes in the EU and NATO) up to? Given the resignation of the military head of the peacekeeping mission in the DRC, one has to wonder whether he found himself in the same position as General Roméo Dallaire in Rwanda in 1994. Then the pressure on him from the UN bureaucrats to resign was only stopped (according to Dallaire himself)[1] by his second in command, a Ghanaian officer, who prevailed on his boss not to give up.

The connection between cheap resources such as coltan, gold, cassiterite, the warring factions and the war must be factored into any attempt to make sense of the current carnage. Yet trying to answer all these questions could take volumes and will not help understand why and how the DRC has arrived at such a point of destruction and self-destruction. There is among most analysts a deep-seated reluctance to look at the visible and invisible legacies of a history that has been, in the main, genocidal and predatory. And not just since 1994.[2]

Looking for the usual culprits at the highest levels of governments and/or multinational corporations is not to ignore those of us who consume the latter's goods. Why don't consumers of computers and cell phones feel compelled not to purchase items that are the result of a well-known criminal process traceable from the extraction of coltan from the eastern DRC? Is their attitude different from that of previous generations who enjoyed the comforts provided by the triangular Atlantic trade and then, later, by colonial occupations? The visible crimes against humanity today have their roots in the refusal to look at the current triumphant economic system as part of the problem. It is not enough to rant against the usual culprits, be they foreign regional leaders or their international supporters. The process that brought the current political leadership to power in the DRC can be traced to, at least, the conditions and circumstances under which independence was achieved in 1960.

As can be seen by the recently unfolding so-called financial crisis, the reluctance to go back in time to the root of the problem is deeply ingrained. It took a long time for pundits and experts alike to mention 1929, and it is still taboo to mention the word depression. Yet history, one should know now, is not unlike nature: it unfolds with warts and all, good and bad, regardless of what historians may wish to edit out. While it is fairly easy to rage and rant against the current cast of regional, national and international leaders for their unrelenting determination to 'do away with the DR Congo', and enrich themselves in the process, a mixture of fear and shame seems to stand in the way of going further back in time in our history. We are ashamed as we understand that we should never have allowed Patrice Emery Lumumba to be overthrown, assassinated and disposed of in an acid bath. Lumumba's elimination was meant to be exemplary in its terrorising effect on the Congolese people. In the subsequent decades, everything was done to ensure that no political leadership inspired by emancipatory politics would emerge. And it seems to have worked far beyond the expectations of its sponsors.

In three years time, on 17 January 2011, it will be the 50th anniversary of the 'successful' killing of Lumumba. The same mentality has been at work trying to balkanise the DRC. Like Lumumba's body, they would like to dissolve it. As with Lumumba, as with colonial rule and slavery earlier, the recipe, in Africa and beyond for dealing with persons, groups or even a country which refuses to conform, has been the same: do away with it. How many Congolese know of Kimpa Vita being burnt at the stake on 2 June 1706, simply for having denounced the Kongo king for allowing slave raiding. In turn Capuchin missionaries denounced her for being a heretic. That was two centuries before Simon Kimbangu's resistance against economic, political and religious colonialism. Imprisoned in 1921, he died in prison in 1951. Done away with.

The same dominant mentality led to the erasure of Yugoslavia from the map. Similar processes are going on in various parts of the planet. The targets may not necessarily be access to cheap resources, but at the core, the doing away with objective is to target people whose will to be free refuses to bend to the dogma of a fundamentalist ideology rooted in the notion that economic liberty must be defended at all cost, regardless of the genocidal sequences left in its path.

For those who might falter in the belief that capitalism is the 'best economic system man has invented', they should read the lead article of *The Economist* (18 October 2008) titled 'Capitalism at bay'. Unsurprisingly, the subtitle is 'What went wrong and, rather more importantly for the future, what did not.' At the end of the very first paragraph, one reads 'Ever since [165 years ago] *The Economist* has been on the side of economic liberty.' Economic liberty has obviously worked wonders for those who fashioned and benefited most from it, starting all the way from slavery. In all of its subsequent manifestations and so-called self-corrections, those who most benefited have maintained their grip on how it should be run, while allowing a few more into the privileged circle.

The prizing of economic liberty over everything else has taken such a toll that it keeps at bay those who might wish to calculate its costs. Could it be that the fear might stem from what might be found? The calculation of human suffering is impossible. In the case of Africa, humanitarianism has been used to alleviate the conscience of those who swear and live by the fruits of economic liberty. As has been seen with the so-called financial crisis, the dominant mindset will always find ways of extracting profits even where it might be thought impossible. The financial engineering acrobatics that have brought about the current crisis have been used before against segments of humanity that had been ruled out of humanity. How many Africans, for example, know that from 1685 to 1848 France applied Le Code Noir as the legal tool for how to treat Africans?[3] The abolition of slavery did not change the habits which had been ingrained in the populace which benefited from slavery. It would be more appropriate to speak of the modernisation of slavery. The financial engineers of those times, with the help of the steam engine, figured that more money could be made by the abolition of slavery and, to boot, give themselves moral accolades for putting an end to something that was not morally sustainable. It never entered the minds of most abolitionists that those they called slaves saw themselves as part of humanity.

France passed the Taubira law in 2001. The law stated that slavery was a crime against humanity. Given what happened at the UN Conference Against Racism and Intolerance in August and September 2001, France's naming of slavery as a crime against humanity was certainly a positive step, but ever since a backlash has been brewing and broke out into the open with historian Pierre Nora's blunt reaction against the law.[4]

This detour may seem irrelevant to what is going on in eastern DRC. It is not, because it reveals how difficult it is to transform a mindset borne from genocidal sequences (wiping out of indigenous populations in the Caribbean and the Americas followed by hunting for slaves in Africa). Segments of humanity benefited immensely from slavery and the slave trade. In the case of Haiti, France and its allies went even further and insisted on payment of compensation to the slave owners and plantation owners. Such compensation was paid from 1825 to 1946. When President Aristide insisted that such payment should be given back, France, including some of its best-known liberal voices, baulked. They then did everything to do away with President Jean-Bertrand

Aristide. Luckily, unlike Toussaint L'Ouverture and Lumumba, he survived. But among those who kept calling for his return, such as Lovinsky Pierre-Antoine, the doing away machine went to work: Lovinsky 'disappeared' in August 2007. His crime was fearlessness and fidelity to the truth process and wanting to bring about change.[5]

The lessons of what happens when humanity and its living principles are trampled on and broken, for example by genocide, have still not been learned. The corrections, whether at Nüremberg or in South Africa, have always been far below what was being called for. The same happened with the Rwanda genocide of 1994. To this day, the unfolding of feminicide (destroying women at their most vulnerable and intimate) in the eastern DRC and the collateral maiming and killing of children are the direct continuation of a refusal to attend to what happened, at all levels, inside and outside Africa. And, of course, this refusal is, in turn, connected to the wider and deeper refusal to face crimes against humanity where and when they happen. The result can be observed today, almost like a spectacle. The inventory of atrocities committed seems endless both in terms of numbers and intensity.

The pattern of 'doing away with' is not peculiar to the DRC. There continues to be a deliberate 'doing away with' people like the pygmies, immigrants, women, children, people with disabilities, workers, the poor, peasants. On a larger and deeper scale, the spectacle of 'doing away with' the planet is unfolding with impunity. By calling it a financial crisis, the leadership of the most advanced economies defined those who must come to the table to discuss how to get out of it. According to the defenders of economic liberty *über alles*, those who have been at the receiving end of its ravages over the centuries must be kept out of the discussion.

In the conference that is being called in Nairobi, there will be nobody representing the women who were raped, and no one will represent the children. The NGOs present there will follow the protocol dictated by the modernisers of the Berlin Conference. Then it was about carving up the continent between those who made themselves count. The mindset at work in Berlin in 1884–85, with regard to Africa, has not changed. Some day it will, because it has to, if humanity is going to survive.

Notes

1. See the documentary on the 10th anniversary of the Rwanda genocide, made by Frontline: www.pbs.org/wgbh/pages/frontline/shows/ghosts/.

2. See, for example, Adam Hochschild's book *King Leopold's Ghost*.

3. See Louis Sala-Molins, *Le code noir ou le calvaire de Canaan* (Presses Universitaires de France, Paris, 2002). Obviously, we are not referring to academics, but even with them, knowing and doing something about it are two different things.

4. See the article by Pierre Nora 'Liberté pour l'histoire' and Christiane Taubira's response 'Mémoire, histoire et droit', in *Le Monde*, 10 and 15 October, 2008 respectively.

5. After Lumumba's assassination, a process of what could be called ideological cleansing led to the doing away of anyone who was considered a Lumumbist. These included people who came from the same region as his birthplace.

6

Hungry for a voice: the food crisis, the market, and socio-economic inequality

Co-authored with Diamantino Nhamposa

4 December 2008

In order to live, one needs to eat; and in order to live, one needs more than just food. In a world ruled by worshippers of the market, it has come to be accepted that principles of justice and solidarity will take second place to everything else. Indeed, that is why one hears more and more often of the distinction between justice and social justice – as if calling for the former will not automatically cover those most affected by the growing disappearance of justice and equality.

Given the current mentality, dominated by greed, selfishness, and selfish charity, it is worth remembering a few cautionary principles: beware of the names that are given to a problem or a disease or a person without the consent of that person. Always remember the Arawaks and those who welcomed Christopher Columbus and his party on what Columbus called Hispaniola. The Arawaks soon died of hunger and disease after welcoming the Europeans. Always remember those who resisted the conquest of their land because they were defending much more than their land. To remember requires much more than mining memories and archives; it will take listening with loving attention to the voices which tend to be ignored, to poets, to those who did die of hunger, to those who would like to speak for themselves as they are, whoever they are (Pygmies, !kung, or Hazabe).

As Ernest Wamba dia Wamba has pointed out, at times like these it is crucial to hear how ordinary people (e.g., people living in forests or deserts) understand food security. For example, among the Kongo in the Democratic Republic of Congo, earth is a package of food and medicine provided by God so people can face hunger and illness. During slavery (in the USA), slave masters sometimes wondered how Africans survived without access to what the masters considered food. It did not occur to the latter that the Africans managed to invent more nutritious food than their masters.

The food crisis is not just about food; it is about understanding humanity and its relation to nature. How the issue is framed or problematised will determine the process of rethinking and finding a solution that is satisfactory primarily to those who have suffered the most from the predatory nature of the current and triumphant economic and financial system. For Wamba dia Wamba, 'it is the destruction of Mother Earth and the building of walls between people and Mother Earth which is at the centre of the food crisis. In the process Mother Earth is transformed, sterilised and turned into the mother of profits for the rich. For the victims it is unconscionable that food should be destroyed in order to increase prices, make people suffer while generating huge profits for the destroyers of Mother Earth.'[1]

Setting the parameters

The current food crisis in the midst of a multiple crisis should provide a wake-up call for all those who are trying to provide solutions by focusing only on food. At first glance, there are at least two competing narratives: one set by those who have run the world and their allies, and the other by those who are expected to submit and accept the word of the self-appointed masters of the world. Formally speaking, the former set their own agendas, via the G8 and the yearly Davos meetings among other places. Those who are expected to submit are reduced to using the United Nations and its specialised agencies, and the World Social Forum. Soon the Security Council and its permanent members will be changed, but it will not matter since the G8 and Davos meetings have ensured that the decisions which do matter to them will no longer be taken within the UN system.

In other words, it is not only in justice, health or, more prosaically, air travel, that the class system has imposed itself; there is justice and health for the poor and justice and health for the rich.

Indeed, if one looks more carefully, it is not difficult to detect that the super rich would like to separate themselves from the rest. But, no matter how hard they would like to distinguish themselves from the rest of humanity, there is only one humanity. Splitting it apart – as the atom was split – willl yield worse results than the process which led to Hiroshima and Nagasaki. Still, more than 50 years later, how many are willing, like Dwight McDonald, to see the dropping of those atomic bombs as the modernisation of Auschwitz and Dachau? Given what happened in the Second World War (and, more importantly, in the centuries leading up to it), shouldn't one ask if the current crises are the by-product of the same competition-to-death mentality which gave rise in several of the most economically advanced countries to a political leader-ship that saw nothing wrong with getting rid, once and for all, of any racially defined group (be it Africans, Asians, Armenians, pygmies, Jews, Tutsi, Hutu)? Asking the question does not mean that one knows the answer. When one can see that the mindset of those genocidal times is still vibrant, it would be irresponsible not to ask questions like, who are the slaves, who are the Jews, who are the colonised? Asking these questions will help uncover, along the way, how poverty and hunger are created, who named them and why they are so named.

The mindset which has trampled humanity under different names – slavery, colonisation, holocaust, apartheid – has not retreated; it has grown like a cancer, destroying the living prin-ciple. At the same time, it passes itself off under names which disguise its lethal, predatory nature, such as biotechnology, which presents itself as promoting life when it is engaged in the process of killing, brutally, softly, and all the ways in between. Biotechnology is a misnomer; given the antecedents, its proper name should be thanato-technology: to live on Planet Earth according to death principles. The chain toward self-destruction has no end: to rape, to enslave, to colonise, to seek the final solu-tion, to bantustanise, to ethnically cleanse a country. Humanity has yet to see the end of its genocidal tendencies and sequences. Under the previous submission processes, the responsibility could be traced back to some sort of state authority, but with sub-mission to the market's rules, responsibility and authority seems to be nowhere and everywhere.

Peoples and nations have been enslaved and colonised by other nations, but at the core of the process, the rules of the market have reigned supreme. The capitalist market has superseded all previous conquering, enslaving, and colonising mechanisms. Indeed, unlike the empires of old, the market (as guided by capitalist principles) has modernised (automated) the mechanisms of domination in ways imperial powers could never have dreamed of achieving. Through market mechanisms, a few former slaves or a few former colonised could become part of the ruling cliques, and in so doing move away from the miseries of hunger and poverty. In times when denunciations of corruption have become a perpetual mantra, the sweet murmurs of the market and the promise of greater wealth to be made through its labyrinths, gag and/or muffle the few voices trying to change course. Before trying to restrict the food crisis to the last few decades and to the usual culprits, one should revisit the histories of those who (since the inauguration of capitalism a few centuries ago) died of hunger in times when the words 'food crisis' were not even uttered[2] – at least not in the manner one hears them today.

Increasingly, food is only accessible through the market, as is work, education, health, justice, birth, the right to exist, the right to breath clean air, and the right to drink clean water. Everything which goes into making life worth living, into making it worth being a human being, is only accessible through mechanisms controlled by a few individuals, but above all by a mindset which is accountable to nobody. The market fundamentalists might say that this is an exaggeration, that they are just as interested in the above objectives as anyone else. As fundamentalists who have benefited from the market, understandably, their primary objective has been, is, and will be to maintain the prism of the market as key determinant in assessing life's value. If the food crisis is not problematised from within this situation, the histories of those who have starved because of who they were (i.e., dispensable), then the exercise is more than likely to provide solutions only beneficial to the so-called 'discoverers' of hunger and famine. Historically, the discoverers (with rare exceptions, like Bartholomeu de las Casas) have never seen themselves, at least initially, as the possible and probable source of the socio-economic problems which are now affecting more than 90 per cent of the world's population.[3]

By discussing the current food crisis from the perspective of the last few decades, these very short-term analysts, consciously or unconsciously, are saying that the problem is momentary and conjunctural. It is neither and has been in the making for a very long time.[4] Sometimes, like now, the time span can be even shorter because of the emphasis on the concomitant financial, energy, and ecological crises. This essay would like to address the current food crisis from a perspective which goes back to at least 1491. As Charles Mann has pointed out, 1492 as the starting point of a post-1492 narrative tends to give the impression that prior to 1492 there was nothing worth remembering.[5] The dominant mindset which emerged out of the so-called discoveries emphasises only the positive aspects, to the exclusion of any aspect which might blemish its record.[6]

The term 'consciousness of evil' is one which has been used to describe what happened during and after the Second World War. Fifty years later, one has slowly but irresistibly, slid into a situation leading to the eradication of people who stand in the way of the total and complete triumph of the will of the richest people of the earth. When Native Americans were driven out of their land, when they lost the material basis of their way of living, they died of hunger and disease. Centuries later, on a bigger scale, masses of people are being starved, while a few are stuffing themselves to death:[7] some, because they are not eating the proper food, others because they just overeat, excited, driven by never ending advertising campaigns. This killing, anti-humanity mindset has reached such a level of intensity that those who are its victims fail to grasp that they do not have to submit to it. All it would take is affirming humanity and the living principles.

The starved's point of view

From way back, if one is willing to listen carefully to the historical echoes of those who screamed against inhumanity, one can hear something like the following:

When people were punished through starvation they protested, but who were they? Slaves. They responded: We are not slaves, we are Africans who were enslaved. For having spoken, they were killed.

The generic human being protested. The screams were heard, but she was a colonial subject. She was jailed, raped, sent to exile only for having spoken when she was supposed to keep silent.

The human being protested, babies, children, old men and women. Protested. Followed by animals, birds, nature. Life protested against death. To no avail. The market must prevail, keeps prevailing, is kept prevailing. The most powerful so dictated.

The habit of not listening to human beings less powerful. The habit of raping with impunity. Led to humanitarianism, a discovery aimed at covering up crimes against humanity. By those who had refused to listen to humanity. And lost their humanity.

From Columbus to today, the discoverers have not changed. They changed tunes to reinforce their mindset, leading one to ask: Was their discovery of humanitarianism a diversion or a negation of their own humanity?

Or are they saying there is a humanity? To be understood, represented, or defended – by them or their agents – through humanitarianism, charitably. And there is a humanity, a humanity against which no crime must be committed.

They discovered themselves as the best representatives of humanity. But they are disconnected from humanity. They have never known starvation. The only thing they understand is how to make money out of their discoveries. Whatever their names: land, slaves, colonies, poverty, misery, hunger.

The history has been known for a long time, but it keeps being pushed back, even when, one should say especially when, it manages to free itself from the shackles of the dominant mindset. An enslaved person who frees herself without waiting for the master's abolition or a colonised people which decolonises itself before it is considered appropriate by the coloniser will be 'taught a lesson'. From Saint-Domingue/Haiti to Indochina/Vietnam, to Cuba, to Kenya, to the DR Congo, to Mozambique, the lesson has been drilled with all the means at the disposal of the dominant mindset, from extreme violence to extreme seduction. The objective is the same: to ensure that fear and/or shame will prevent the descendants of those who tried the impossible (and succeeded) from every trying again to free themselves. More on shame further below.

Identifying and addressing the deepest roots

If the current food crisis is going to be resolved for the benefit of those who have been most affected by its unfolding, and in a way that allows them to participate in deciding how to remove hunger, then the food crisis must be examined far and away beyond the rattling of statistical tables which reveal nothing more than the obvious – that the poorest of the poor[8] have been getting poorer and poorer for the benefit of the richest of the rich. For as long as humanity has existed the former have risen against the latter, but one must resist the temptation of agreeing that emancipatory politics will always fail. One must also resist the more recent temptation of accepting the notion that thoughts expressed by highly educated intellectuals count more than the thoughts of uneducated or poorly educated peasants. Being uneducated does not mean that one is incapable of thinking. The Africans who overthrew slavery in Saint Domingue/Haiti knew better than those who predicted that they could not possibly achieve such a feat. It is not difficult to imagine the slave owners (and the Enlightenment philosophers) saying to whoever would listen: What do the slaves know about freedom?

Yet, these were the very people who, having dared against all odds and all predictions of failure, left us with lessons on how to achieve freedom. But again, the lessons retold by the discoverers and their descendants and their allies will always differ from the ones recounted, remembered by the so-called 'discovered' and their descendants and their allies. More often than not, one finds among the latter the most vociferous distorters of the histories and lessons emerging from battles against those who defend submission to the dominant mindset. For example, listening to the history of Haiti as recounted by C.L.R. James or, more recently, Peter Hallward is not the same as hearing it from Alex Dupuy.[9] The richest of the rich have multiple ways of enforcing their views, but so too do the poorest of the poor, provided they are convinced that they can.

For any human being, suffering can reach an unbearable point. But at the same time, over and over in history, people have shown a heroic capacity to resist and rise above the most extreme forms of torture, especially when people are motivated by a political understanding of their situation that is disconnected from the idea that the way out can only be through the dominant mindset's way of thinking.

Again if one looks at the history of Haiti, it is easy to understand why the slave and plantation owners would seek, by any means necessary, to prove that the Africans who overthrew slavery on Saint Domingue should never have tried: financial, economic, political, religious, cultural, and intellectual means were used to convey the message that the inhabitants of Saint Domingue would have been better off had they not risen against slavery. In a nutshell, everything has been done to ensure that other enslaved Africans (or those enslaved by any subsequent system) reconsider emancipatory politics as a viable option.

The history of Haiti is one of the most exemplary for both sides of the ideological fence separating emancipatory and consensual/ submissive/abolitionist politics.

Fear of one's history and fear of hunger

From the historical record, it is known that the turnover ratio of Africans in Saint Domingue was very high. Supply was cheap and less costly than seeking to improve maintenance. It was cheaper to get fresh bodies and use them to death. The demographic ratio was also favourable to the Africans, free and enslaved ones. From the beginning to the end of the 18th century, the number of Africans went from around 2,000 to about half a million. As in any such situation, a range of possibilities must have been discussed: improve the conditions of work/treatment, including better food, or get rid of the system altogether.

However, before going further in our examination, it is important to connect the history of Africans in Saint Domingue and Africans from one of their geographical points of origin: the Kongo kingdom. Only 85 years (about three generations) separate two events related to the overthrow of slavery. On 2 July 1706, Kimpa Vita (some times known as Dona Beatriz) was burned at the stake for having tried to convince the Kongo king to put an end to the activities of the Portuguese slave raiders and traders. This was not just a one-person enterprise. Those who agreed with her denunciations rallied behind a movement known as the

Antonian movement, so called because Kimpa Vita said that she had received her message from St Anthony. Little is known about the movement following the death of Kimpa Vita, but it is not unreasonable to surmise that memories of the movement survived and may have influenced those who in 1791 in Saint Domingue decided and vowed to end slavery. And, it would not be unfair to presume that, as a principle, humanity has genes which are allergic to any form of slavery. From within humanity there are always going to be those pushing for emancipatory politics.

The Africans who ended up in Saint Domingue lived in a most fearsome situation. In order to understand their determination to do away with slavery, one should try to understand what slavery was about.[10] This is almost impossible, regardless of the descriptions available through historical, fictional, or cinematographic accounts.[11] The use of an entire continent as a hunting ground for enslaving people is the kind of trespassing against humanity which, because it has remained unacknowledged, opened the door to the committing of further offences, not just in terms of the number of people maimed, slaughtered, and raped but also because it further reinforced the mindset that competition-to-death, by any means, is the most efficient way of organising any economy. One can never stress enough that unless the enormity of what happened is eventually understood, it will be impossible to do anything about the current challenges faced by humanity.[12]

Out of this mindset has grown the habit of disregarding or erasing what the industrial enslavement of an entire continent has done. Such a process of slowly minimising, muffling, or eradicating the efforts of those who stood up against a crime against humanity – long before it was denounced by the 'discoverers' – ends up distorting any attempt to rise up against some of its most damaging consequences. This minimising of slavery and its consequences has been repeated at every subsequent transition (for example, at the end of the colonial period and the end of apartheid).

When the French government passed the legislation recognising slavery as a crime against humanity (Loi Christiane Taubira, 2001),[13] it was done in a way which was aimed at shielding those who collectively benefited from slavery. How else should one interpret the French government's behaviour toward President Jean-Bertrand Aristide in 2004? The kidnapping was carried out by the American military in collaboration with the French and Canadian governments and their allies, including the Central African Republic. The whole episode reminded one, more than 200 years later, of the kidnapping of Toussaint l'Ouverture.

It might be asked what is the meaning of this long detour into the history of Haiti for the purpose of confronting the current food crisis. It has to do with resisting the attempt to frame the food crisis from the perspective of those who want to benefit the most from it. In its most simplistic terms, the food crisis is being analysed and explained within the parameters put in place by a dominant mindset which has its deepest roots in how it organised the pauperisation of those who had defeated the biggest scourge of those times. Indeed, it was more than a scourge; it was the embryo of what was to become known under globalisation two centuries later.

The Africans, then, understood their situation without political or charitable representatives. Their understanding of how to get out of their situation was arrived at through their own thinking and, certainly, without the help of the Enlightenment philosophers. The French Revolution of 1789 had taken place and helped bring forward the idea, at least among some, that if the banner of Liberty, Fraternity and Equality was going to have any meaning, then it had to lead to the complete and total abolition of slavery. However, there were massive efforts, not just in France but also in England and Spain, to try and reverse what the Africans had done. The abolition of slavery in French-controlled territories would not take place till 1848, which a century later would see the Universal Declaration of Human Rights. But as stated above, these rights apply differently depending on whether one belongs to humanity (first class) or to humanity-existing-through-humanitarianism (second and third classes).

Will the food crisis be resolved according to the discriminatory perspective above or according to an understanding that there is only one humanity? In other words, will the question of how to eradicate hunger and poverty be posed by those whose dominant mindset has generated massive hunger and poverty, or will the poor and the hungry frame the questions and provide the answers without the humanitarian or charitable advice of the 'discoverers' of poverty and hunger?

It is not difficult to see that the food crisis is connected to other crises – economic, financial (the so-called credit crunch) and climatic change. It is also clear that all institutions have been mobilised, from those with apparently appropriate knowledge on the issue (e.g., the Food and Agricultural Organisation (FAO) and government ministers) to personalities like the former UN Secretary General Kofi Anan, who understand the seriousness and gravity of the crisis. But when all of these specialists meet and discuss, the voices of peasants, the voices of those who produce food, either for themselves and their families or for corporations, are rarely, if ever heard. Moreover, how can people whose mind-sets are responsible for the food crisis be expected to provide satisfactory answers? How can people who see nothing wrong in their mindset be expected to get rid of, or distance themselves from, the very way of thinking which has brought the inhabitants of the planet face-to-face with permanent disaster?

The fear at work in the minds of the above group is not the same as the one to be found among those who belong to the most vulnerable inhabitants of the planet. A mind which does not have to worry about eating three meals a day, nor about providing food for all members of its family, can be at peace while those who go hungry on a daily basis often resort to suicide as the solution to their daily miseries.[14] An inconvenient question arises which is not unlike the one which arose with regard to the HIV/AIDS epidemic: Could it be that the richest of the rich would rather let the hungry die than discuss with them the best way to resolve the crisis?

Fear and shame: consciousness of evil or consciousness of shame?

In addition to fear there is shame. While psychologists have studied how to detect people who are lying, there has been lit-tle interest in trying to understand why and how, individually and collectively, human beings are eager to hide anything which might be shameful. The fear of having a shameful act revealed to all provides a powerful incentive to hide.[15]

How a segment of humanity has treated others in the past can lead to a sense of shame and the desire to ask for forgiveness. Unfortunately, one is not operating under conditions which are levelled: those who know from their own historical records that they have perpetrated shameful acts are not eager to bring them to the surface. What was done to Africans and to Native Americans by other people in the name of a way of thinking – an ideology, a religion – has been felt unevenly all over the world. In some cases, such as France towards Africans and slavery, it has been acknowledged that slavery is a crime against humanity, but little has been done to reverse the associated direct and indirect consequences. Indeed, a belated apology has often been used as the most efficient way of preserving the gains acquired through the crime.[16]

Once a taboo has been trespassed on, it becomes extremely difficult if not impossible to overcome the direct and indirect consequences. With regard to food, in a world in which people should not go hungry, people do go hungry precisely because it has become acceptable, in a mindset dominated by a dictatorial free market system, that some people are going to die of hunger. The accepted norm, under the present mindset, is that hunger cannot be eradicated, regardless of the efforts. The fact that humanity has been able to eradicate certain diseases, including hunger, is not seen as proof that hunger could be banned.

Why are the histories of Saint Domingue/Haiti more emblematic than ever?

In their self-congratulatory march to the top, the richest of the rich have always feared what the poorest of the poor would or could do if they were to understand their own situations without outside interferences. Along the way, the former segment of humanity has resorted, directly or indirectly, to fearsome practices in order to dominate and/or obliterate those they considered less than human.[17] The process of how Haiti has been impoverished following 1804 is pertinent to our thinking about the current food crisis.

Haiti, for example, used to be self-sufficient in rice, while the DR Congo used to export cassava and many other food commodities. Both countries now have to import thanks to a process which involved World Bank economists' and the US government's common strategy of liberalisation. The process of turning self-sufficient economies into dependent ones has been documented ad infinitum.[18] Aid and charity complement each other as the remedy to the predatory extremes unleashed by the dictatorial rule of competition.[19]

Succeeding where success was not expected, as the Africans did in eradicating slavery, could have inflicted a serious blow to the system.[20] Those who had most benefited from slavery had to impose their own timing: it took another half-century for France to abolish slavery. Timing was crucial in order to tame those who had thought, back then, that slavery was indeed a crime against humanity. Again, as with abolition, the timing of recognition had to be imposed by those who had most benefited from the crime itself. It was only in 2001 that France finally passed a law recognising slavery as a crime against humanity.[21]

While working in Mozambique between 1979 and 1986, I once had a poster against apartheid: 'Apartheid is a Crime against Humanity'. Looking at it a visitor asked what it meant. I remained speechless, thinking it was self-explanatory. How long will it take for the South African government to acknowledge apartheid as a crime against humanity? Or, is it that, in the name of Truth and Reconciliation, the multiple roots of the crime will be silenced?

From 1962 to 1974, the Front for the Liberation of Mozambique (Frelimo) succeeded, against all odds, in putting an end to Portuguese colonial rule. Such a success, as in Haiti, had to be reversed. The context, in Mozambique, was dominated by the Cold War. Frelimo had been supported by the USSR, the People's Republic of China, Cuba, Vietnam, the German Democratic Republic, but also by people from western countries such as Italy, Holland and Sweden. As Henry Kissinger stated during a visit to southern Africa in April 1976, communism had to be defeated in the region.[22] Not long after that, one of the most vicious civil wars, which looked as if it were aimed at 'teaching Frelimo a lesson', began to unfold.

The consequences of the war have been so devastating that, in the name of the peace achieved in 1992, it has become preferable not to speak about the war. So much so that the silence around the civil war is now being extended to the war against the colonisers, as if that was the war which should never have taken place. Again, it is difficult not to think of Haiti and what the Africans did to slavery. Today's elite in Haiti acts as if it wishes slavery had not been abolished, at least not in the manner it was between 1791 and 1804. Today's elite in Mozambique prefers to focus on how to become as rich as possible as quickly as possible, and it is possible that some of them might even be inaudibly saying to themselves that had it not been for Frelimo, they would be much better off today.[23]

Both Haiti and Mozambique are most talked about as very poor countries. Thanks to outside donors, anti-poverty programmes do help the poorest of the poor overcome hunger and other problems. It is understandable that those who suffered the consequences of war (especially the civil war 1980–92) would rather not face that situation again. A question arises though: Should the fear of what happened during colonial rule or after lead to a fear of politics, or fear of thinking for oneself about how best to get out of a situation? Moreover, should the fact that the Soviet Union and all its allies 'lost' the Cold War lead Mozambicans to the conclusion that anything which resembles, directly or indirectly, socialism and/or communism must be banished forever?

The process of enforcing only one way of thinking about colonial rule and its demise has followed the same pattern as the one which has been observed in Haiti: everything must be done so that a different way of organising society, production, and distribution does not emerge. Differences are acceptable if they are not antagonistic towards the dominant way of thinking.

Césaire, poetry, politics and history

When Aimé Césaire passed away recently it dawned on many people, including myself, that someone very special had lived among us who had not been heard or understood as he should have been.[24] This has happened before and will happen again. In the future, some will describe him as a prophetic voice. He always insisted, without putting it like this, that he was not a politician and that his politics were in his poetry.[25] To a specific question by Françoise Vergès on the relationship between his poetry and politics he points out: 'La poésie révèle l'homme à lui-même. Ce qui est au plus profond de moi-même se trouve certainement dans ma poésie. Parce que ce 'moi-même', je ne le connais pas. C'est le poème qui me le révèle et même l'image poétique.'[26] ('It is poetry which reveals the human being to itself. What comes from deepest within myself can be found in my poetry. Because even this self of mine, I do not know. It is the poem which reveals it to me, even the poetic imagery.' [My translation])

Using statistical data to demonstrate the insanity and the injustices behind the current food crisis will not make a dent in the consciousness of those who are responsible for it. For someone like Césaire – and Françoise Vergès is right to emphasise this point[27] – the immensity of the wound inflicted by one segment of humanity onto another, through slavery and later compounded by colonisation, has never been assessed. Such an assessment is deliberately avoided because of the fear and shame of what would happen to all those who only know one truth, one history: the history, the truth of humanity seen through the eyes and the mindset of those who have enslaved, who have colonised. The resulting shock of discovering what had been hidden could be overwhelming to those who are unprepared.

From within this kind of historical narrative, the dominant mindset is bound to present access to food, health, education, and justice as something which is easily available to anyone provided it is so desired. To paraphrase Françoise Vergès, the dominant mindset (in France) is convinced that the 1848 abolition of slavery was France's gift to the Africans. This paternalistic mindset is as deeply embedded today as it was in 1848. Enslavement to the dominant system is being carried out by different means, but the results are just as devastating for humanity as a whole. The direct and indirect consequences of slavery and colonisation have never been dealt with. As a result, one hears calls to the poor to change their attitude. It is very easy to promote the idea that the poor are poor because they want to be poor, just as it is easy to accuse peasants of laziness. No one among the richest of the rich ever accuses the land stealer, the bankers, the speculators of being lazy, even though, most of the time, their robbing is conducted from comfortable offices.[28]

From Aimé Césaire's poetry one has heard, but not yet learned, that living is an art. The food speculators, the financiers, the colonisers, the enslavers, and all those who have never seen anything wrong in their mindset, or in living as an accounting exercise, may praise our beloved Césaire and even quote from his poetry, but they will do so from within the accounting mindset, willing to accept him paternalistically, just as they accepted the abolition of slavery in 1848. As stated in the preamble, the food crisis is one of the multiple manifestations of humanity approaching a dead end.

More and more members of humanity are beginning to sense that when living principles determined by human beings are being superseded by principles anonymously determined by a deity called the Market, then something, somewhere, has gone wrong. When food such as corn or maize is being produced for reasons other than to feed people, then surely it is a sign that the segment of humanity which promotes this diversion of foodstuffs has modernised exponentially, as happened during the Second World War. For the sake of defending or promoting a mindset, masses of people are being reduced to a status of non-existence.

Freedom without equality and fraternity is freedom to annihilate

The market, unfettered of any rules based on equality and fraternity between all segments of humanity, can only lead to the annihilation of humanity. This is not a prediction. It is happening as surely as the melting of the ice caps at both poles, as surely as global warming is progressing. How does one reverse a mindset which has taken hold not just of the speculators, bankers, political, and religious leaders, but of ordinary people around the world? How does one defeat the deeply rooted tendency to think that the task at hand is impossible?

For one, the voices which have been saying the same things for centuries must be heard and acted upon. It is not enough to say that humanity is one if we simultaneously refuse to listen to some of the voices, never mind the reasons. When the crisis is as serious as the current one, regardless of the angle from which it is tackled, is it not wise to acknowledge that every single member of humanity has a say? Should one not call on and encourage the tiniest voices to rise? Isn't the wisest course to accept, in the face of inconvenient truths, the inconvenient truths uttered for past centuries by the poorest of the poor?

When confronted with the systematic denial of one's humanity, there is only one possible course: to stand up against such a
denial. It is crucial that resistance against the dominant mindset
be conducted from within the principles aimed at a different
mindset. It must be firmly grounded on solidarity. The only force
to be used will be the force of art, poetry and science at the service
of humanity.

Artists, poets and scientists must eat too. Freedom by itself
does not feed, but freedom with equality and fraternity can.
Artists, poets and scientists do not have to congregate in places
designated by the market promoters. In such places, all voices
shall be heard, provided they respect the basic principles to be
agreed upon by those who insist on the necessity to change the
mindset. Here are some possible principles:

- Food producers and the poorest of the poor must be heard in
  their own voices
- The multiplicity of the voices calling for emancipatory politics
  must be accepted
- No representation will be accepted
- Each voice must heard from where it is, as it is.

These are by no means the only principles that could be considered.

Healing from fear and shame

The transition from apartheid, even with the help of the Truth and
Reconciliation Commission (TRC), has not lived up to its heralded
promises. The May 2008 pogroms against the poorest of the poor
by other poorest of the poor has revealed the shortcomings of
the TRC as a panacea. It has also brought out very sharply the
shortcomings of the African National Congress (ANC), both the
party and the government, in educating the population about the
international support without which apartheid would not have
been defeated. In that education, the role of ordinary Africans
who risked their lives and generously gave all they could should
have been highlighted. This failure, however, must be shared by
most African governments because of their common tendency
to disregard the role of ordinary people in the making of their

histories. The failure to inform and educate must also be shared by those who, during apartheid, remained silent and profited. As has been remarked, it sometimes sounds now as though during apartheid everyone in South Africa was resistant to it.

As with all previous major transitions (from slavery to post-slavery, from colonialism to post-colonialism), the defeated side quickly reorganises itself with the objective of minimising its losses. In that process they are helped by their previous enemies (now referred to as adversaries). As in Nkrumah's famous motto, the defeated side is convinced that once the political kingdom has been seized, the rest will follow. Yet, in social and economic terms, they find themselves suddenly distant from the very individuals and groups who have made it possible to seize the kingdom and much closer to their previous enemies, whose main thinking was focused on how to keep the economy going as well as before. Whether it was in the post-colonial or post-apartheid eras, the previous masters' understanding of how to keep the economy growing prevailed. One of the results, especially, but not only, in South Africa, has been increasing violence

In South Africa, the new government's fear made them determined to show that things in the country would be different from what had happened in the rest of the continent. That fear led the ANC leadership to move away from the Freedom Charter, even from the creative principles to provide the poorest of the poor with genuine rewards and, more importantly, a say in transforming politics.

As pointed out by the members of Abahlali baseMjondolo, to have a say in transforming politics meant, among other things, speaking for themselves and not being represented by politicians. The poorest of the poor who live in shacks in Durban, Johannesburg, and Cape Town see themselves as the ones who are really defending the principles contained in the Freedom Charter. Democracy means that everyone thinks, that everyone deserves respect and dignity. Freedom must mean that when decent housing, and decent living conditions are not provided for the poor, they are the best qualified to make sure that their voices are heard, clearly without translators or intermediaries, be they lawyers, municipality leaders, university lecturers, politicians.[29]

The similarities between what the poorest of the poor and

peasants are suffering across the world call for a reinforcement of already existing links, and for greater sharing of the stories and histories of resistance against what Amit Bhaduri has referred to as the TINA syndrome (There Is No Alternative to globalisation).[30] This syndrome is not new. The imposition of colonial rule was presented as an altruistic exercise, bringing civilisation to Africa. Forced labour was presented as an educational exercise.

Emancipatory politics must go hand in hand with emancipatory historical narratives and move away from narratives framed by the so-called success stories of globalisation which are told from the perspective of multinational mega corporations and the financial institutions at their service.

Notes

1. Personal communication from Professor Ernest Wamba dia Wamba, 27 October 2008.

2. At one time, during its triumphant emergence, the Roman empire tried to resolve its food crisis by conquering Egypt.

3. Clearly the situation is more complex than being presented here. By 'discoverer', I do not just mean people like Columbus, but also the enslavers, the colonisers, the participants of the Berlin conference, the officials of the most powerful nations in institutions such as the UN, etc.

4. Fernand Braudel, and many others since, rightly insisted on approaching history from a long-term perspective. Unfortunately, such an approach has tended to favour the questions emerging out of the dominant narrative. In the Pambazuka News no. 383 focused on the food crisis, the length of time was even shorter, being limited to the 1970s. If one is going to make sense of the food crisis today, but also try to understand other food crises in the past (e.g., the potato famine in Ireland in the 19th century), the framing of how the crisis has unfolded should be as deep and wide as possible.

5. Charles Mann (2005) *1491: New Revelations of the Americas Before Columbus*, New York, Alfred A. Knopf.

6. For example, Howard Zinn in his *A People's History of the United States: 1492–Present* can only go as far as providing an inventory of the slaughter of the Native Americans and the Africans. For him 1776 is still the event. And as the subtitle indicates, the starting point of his narrative is 1492.

7. See Raj Patel (2007) *Stuffed and Starved, The Hidden Battle for the World Food System*, London, London, Portobello Books.

8. The history of how the poorest of the poor reached this stage has been observed across the planet and for centuries and generations: from food producers, they were forced off their land and reduced to search for work in an environment in which there was only work for a few.

9. C.L.R. James, *The Black Jacobins*; Peter Hallward (2007) *Damming the Flood:*

Haiti, Aristide and the Politics of Containment, Verso; see also Peter Hallward's review of Alex Dupuy's *The Prophet and Power: Jean-Bertrand Aristide, the International Community and Haiti*, Rowan and Littlefield, 2007. http://tinyurl.com/5rgyx6.

10. The importance of this cannot be overstressed in view of the tendency within the dominant mindset to downplay the horrors of slavery. See J. Thornton (1998) *Africa and Africans in the Making of the Atlantic World, 1400–1800*, Cambridge, Cambridge University Press.

11. In his *Black Jacobins*, C.L.R. James did try. Fiction writers have tried, from Ayi Kwei Armah's *Two Thousand Seasons* to Toni Morison's *Beloved*. Haile Gerima in his movie, *Sankofa*, offered a harrowing view of what it was like. Still, when all is said and done, I would argue that no one, to this day and with my greatest respect for the above writers, has come anywhere near to measuring what slavery meant both individually and collectively, especially, but not only, in psychic terms. I have to assume that such measurement, not just in physical terms, will one day be possible. This hope rests, in part, on the realisation that someone somewhere did achieve that impossible act, but that it has not been recorded in the form and/or in the place where it would be noticed. There are exceptions, most notably Aimé Césaire (see) *Nègre je suis, nègre je resterai*, an interview with Françoise Vergès, published in 2005 by Albin Michel, Paris, in particular pages pp. 52–6 and 102–6).

12. A point cogently made by Françoise Vergès in the Césaire book (2005).

13. Its application officially began on 10 May 2004.

14. See Raj Patel (2007) *Stuffed and Starved*, London, Portobello Books.

15. In recent times, it has been possible to see how difficult it is to accept that people in very powerful positions can lie. In earlier times, Hitler and his acolytes found out that a lie repeated a thousand times became a truth.

16. France, among the nations most involved in transatlantic slavery, has probably taken the boldest step by declaring, through the Loi Taubira, that slavery is a crime against humanity. However, this bold step has triggered a sort of blowback against it, particular among historians. See Pierre Nora's 'Liberté pour l'histoire' in *Le Monde* (10 October 2008) and Christiane Taubira's response a few days later: 'Mémoire, histoire et droit' in *Le Monde* (15 October 2008).

17. In May 2008 in South Africa, the poorest of the poor (so-called indigenous South Africans) went on a rampage against the poorest of the poor foreigners. This has been the most recent and exemplary illustration of how entrenched the competitive mindset is. It also reveals the structural shortcomings of the transition from apartheid to post-apartheid founded on the erroneous notion that colouring the richest of the rich in black would radically transform the economic/financial tenets of apartheid days.

18. One of the most interesting accounts has been given by John Perkins in his *Confessions of An Economic Hit Man* (2006) Plume. See also Raj Patel (2007) *Stuffed and Starved*, London, Portobello Books.

19. That it does not have to be so has long ago been proved. See, for example, Marcel Mauss's essay 'Essai sur le don' (1924) and the website of Revue du MAUSS at http://www.revuedumauss.com.

20. What was feared was the effect it could have on other Africans wanting to get rid of slavery in other countries.

21. In 2006, 40 members of the French National Assembly called for the abrogation of the Loi Taubira. See http://tinyurl.com/69m675.

22. Piero Glijeses (2002) *Conflicting Missions: Havana, Washington, and Africa, 1959–1976*, Chapell Hill, University of North Carolina Press.

23. Such inaudible murmuring may even come from the mouths of bona fide veterans of the armed struggle. See Duarte Tembe's book (2000) on Samora: *Samora: O Destino da Memória* Maputo, Ndjira, p. 19. And also the interview given by Jorge Rebelo to the weekly *Savana* (Ericinio Salema and Paola Rolletta) on 6 July 2008. It can be viewed at http://tinyurl.com/6jhq5e.

24. Obviously there are exceptions to this deficiency. There is a difference between knowing someone was special and having understood the true worth of the person. See for example Daniel Maximin's Préface to Césaire's (2008) *Ferrements et autres poèmes*, Editions Points.

25. Aimé Césaire (1996) 'Calendrier laminaire', in Laminaire Moi, *Anthologie Poétique*, Paris, Imprimerie nationale, pp. 233–4; and Aimé Césaire (2005) *Nègre je suis, nègre je resterai. Entretiens avec Françoise Vergès*. Paris, Albin Michel, pp. 47–50.

26. Aimé Césaire (2005) p. 47.

27, Aimé Césaire (2005) pp. 111–36.

28. There are exceptions. Karl Marx being the most prominent one with his reference to 'coupon clipping capitalists'.

29. In his most recent intervention, S'bu Zikode has made these politics very clear. See S'bu Zikode's speech at the Diakonia Economic Justice Forum, 28 August 2008 at http://www.abahlali.org/.

30. See http://www.india-seminar.com/2008/582/582_amit_bhaduri.htm.

7

From Africa to Haiti to Gaza – fidelity to humanity

First, not quite, but we have to start somewhere,
There were the Arawaks, the Caribs and the Amerindians
Then their land became known as Hispaniola,
As Saint Domingue, as the economic jewel
Of French overseas possessions
Thanks to Africans kidnapped, chained, shipped
Processed, codified, stamped as property
While always knowing they belonged
To no one but humanity
And through fidelity to humanity
Turned Saint Domingue into Haiti
Fraternity, equality and liberty
Their only motto
Defeating the obscurantist
Philosophers of the Enlightenment
For thirteen years, 1791–1804
Without support
From humanitarian abolitionists
Defeating the most powerful armies of the day
Spain, England, France
Fidelity to humanity
Their only prescription

Plan B was out of the question
Humanity had to prevail
But its sworn enemy had a plan B:
With lethal vengeance
Napoleon reinstated slavery
Take no prisoners, his motto
Severe, if necessary, capital punishment
Against the trespassers of
Nascent capital yet to be named
Capitalism, the crusher of humanity

With exemplary brutality
Long before the birth of Gaza-upon-Mediterranean
Haiti was turned into the poorest nation
– Gaza-upon-Atlantic –
For having dared simply
To challenge and obsoletify
The Black Code of Louis XIV
Rules of engagement against/for
Slaves balancing terror, torture, fear, death
Ensuring the endurance of slavery
Beyond the monarchy
Thanks to a self-proclaimed emperor
Napoleon Bonaparte the impostor

Plan B prospered so well beyond
Napoleon's dreams of restoring slavery
We may all ask, maybe naively,
Had he known his treatment of Africans
Would later inspire Hitler's
Holocausting of the Jews?

Would he have seen Africans
As humanity and not as property?

Not every French was/is a fan of slavery's restorer:
Taubira Law of 2001 declares
Slavery a Crime Against Humanity
Could it be that France might
Be restoring Fidelity to Humanity?

But could it be too late when
Humanity or those who pretentiously
Speak for it refuse to know
The distinction between
Might and right
Right and wrong
Charity and solidarity

Could it be too late when
Survivors and/or their descendants
Of an unthinkable crime think
The best way to stand up for humanity
Is to slaughter/bomb humanity as deliberately
And brutally smart as possible?

Could it be too late when
Slaughtering humanity
Can be done with impunity
Thanks to a genocided past
As if anything can be traded, erased,
Commodified, genetically modified
To fit a globalised paradise

Where no one will know
The difference between
Gaza-upon-Atlantic
Haiti-upon-Mediterranean
Except for those who vowed
Fidelity to humanity

Can't we see the obvious consequences of
Relentlessly violating humanity
Now Palestinians, then Africans centuries ago
Today displaced, refugees, best fodder
For humanitarian missions
The modernised version of abolitionists
On a mission which has not changed:
Violate humanity,
Eradicate it if too vocal
But Sabra, Shatila can still be heard

Palestinians are full members of humanity
Homelessed in their homeland, denied existence
By all means, constantly searching
For the ultimate way
Of getting rid of them
Their annihilation will not be called
A Crime Against Humanity because,
By definition, it has been repeated forever,
It only happens at Auschwitz, and other
Concentration camps in a World War

Palestinians are like Native Americans
Whose land was taken, whose genocide

Refuses to be called a genocide
Palestinians, Africans interchangeable destinies
Torn from their land, thrown into ships,
Refugeed in strips of land
Enslaved, imprisoned, less than property
Therefore not fit to come under
A Crime Against Humanity

Palestinians, Africans, in the same boat
When the unending story of negating humanity started
Like Africans they are being processed and branded
Fit to be fodder for humanitarian crisis because what is being done
Must not be called
A Crime Against Humanity

For fear of trespassing which taboo?

No one dares to call the slaughter of civilians
In Gaza by its proper name
A Crime Against Humanity

For fear of trespassing which taboo?

From the times of the Arawaks
Violating, torturing, liquidating
Humanity with impunity
Has led to greater and greater
Crimes against humanity
Franchised differently
Preparing the biggest holocaust
Humanity has ever known and,

When that unfolds, as before,
We shall hear the usual
Shameful lame lie
'We did not know'.

8

Born out of genocide; born to live off genocide

September 2005

Capitalism has been so genocidal that it is worthwhile positing that it cannot be otherwise, despite attempts to humanise it. How capitalism came about, how it has been portrayed (by friends and foes) over the centuries but especially now, reinforces the idea that it cannot be done away with. How and where it has slaughtered in massive and horrific ways should be understood as only the smallest manifestation of its genocidal nature – not just against one group of people, but against all human beings. Could it have been otherwise?

Those who are convinced that capitalism can be humanised will argue yes. Unfortunately, the data is so skewed in their favour that to argue the opposite is as huge an obstacle as the challenge faced by the Africans who rose up against slavery in Haiti in 1791. If the above question is going to be discussed adequately, capitalism and its history must no longer be treated as if, by definition, it is immune from evil. The hypothesis is that the principles which have sustained it propagate death. Capitalism kills everything it touches, especially when it claims to do otherwise. It has devised as many ways of killing as there are declared and undeclared worshippers.

Capitalism and how victims of genocides become killers

Self-appointed certifiers of evil can easily be blind to their own actions. For former US Secretary of State Madeleine Albright, the death of half a million children in Iraq as a result of US imposed sanctions was considered 'worth' the effort. Yet, why does it seem easier to accept the description of a Hutu machete-

wielding genocider as beyond barbarism? It is as if certain epi-
thets and words can only be linked to certain peoples. Yet, victims
of genocides can easily become killers – more easily than can be
imagined. In its history of always imposing its principles, rules
and laws, capitalism will eventually face the very practices it has
attributed to its enemies.

As capitalism inaugurated itself, about 500 years ago, so it has
continued to reproduce itself, modernising its ways and refining
how it sells itself. The current occupation of Iraq is a modernised,
updated visual illustration of how Amerindians were stripped
of their land and how Africans and Asians were yanked from
their homes and land by what came to be known initially as The
System – meaning slavery and all that grew out of it.

There is a tendency, even among the most critical voices (e.g.
Howard Zinn's *History of the United States*), not to see the connections between what could be described as the inaugural homelessness of the Amerindians and the Africans, Hitler's *lebensraum*,
today's homelessness in the richest countries of the planet and the
same phenomenon in the streets of Fallujah, Palestine and South
Africa. At this rate, for how long will humanity be able to call
Planet Earth home?

I do not claim to say anything new. Many have said it
before, more eloquently, forcefully and inspiringly (e.g. Fredy
Perlman, *Against His-tory, Against Leviathan*; Bertram Gross,
Friendly Fascism). The tradition of resisting the system did not
just start from 19th century Europe, as it included those who left
no writings, but screamed and fought like hell against their kin
predators. It has included the survivors of certified and uncerti-
fied holocausts. It must include the voices which continue to be
silenced because their suffering did not register on the Richter
scale of genocidal certification, and remain stubbornly unacknowledged. Repetition, in different multiple ways, can be helpful in strengthening resistance to capitalism, in its terrorising and/
or user-friendly forms. For example, the well-known genocidal
sequences of the 20th century have been identified (and certified)
in ways which, in one stroke, exempt and anonymise the real cul-
prit from closer scrutiny.

'Never Again' applied selectively

And, if the famous 'Never Again' should really be stood by, it is necessary to look at capitalism with less benevolent, opportunistic eyes simply because the pillars of power today (military, economic, political, juridical, cultural and religious) have been moulded by the manner in which capitalism emerged and sees itself as angelic, in triumphal colours. One of the measures (and by no means the only one) of how total the triumph has been can be seen, most recently, in how the current US administration is forcing the nation-state signatories of environmental and international criminal laws to retreat from signed agreements, whether in Geneva, Kyoto or Rome. But then, this ignoring of international conventions and covenants is not new, as, for example, can be seen today in the way the Convention Against Genocide (1948) has been ignored by the signatories.

Globalisation as portrayed today by the G8 has been sold in the same fashion over the last 500 years: through a combination of military conquests, territorial occupation, minimal social and humanitarian programmes, corruption, severe and protracted punishment for those who, collectively or individually, do not submit (e.g. Haiti, Cuba, Grenada, Nicaragua, Lumumba, Malcolm X, Martin Luther King, Leonard Peltier, Mumia Abu Jamal, to mention only a few).

By definition, capitalism carries within it an unrelenting need for total control not just of the market, but of everything, of life and death. There is no other morality or ethics but the triumph of the power principle: 'might is right'. 'Never Again' cannot just apply to the Second World War Holocaust, but must be linked to the genocidal sequences unleashed by capitalism, otherwise, 'Never Again' will never apply (or ever so selectively, as has been the practice).

From slavery until today, the system has been regularly updated and modernised. In times of crisis, when its real nature is difficult to hide, capitalism takes on a reformist mantle as it did through the abolition of slavery, or in other transitional phases, such as from colonial rule, or from apartheid in South Africa.

To those who argue that what we are seeing is no different from how previous empires have come and gone, one can only say that it is the first time in history that humans have mastered the capacity to instantly destroy all life on the planet. From the end of the Second World War, or more precisely, since Hiroshima and Nagasaki, efforts have been made to control the proliferation of nuclear weapons. Those efforts have failed, are failing and will continue to fail unless the deep, rarely acknowledged causes which led to the First World War, the Second, the Third (the so-called Cold War) and the Fourth World War (worldwide structural adjustment programmes which have come full circle to the US via the attempt to do away with social security) and now the Fifth World War (the current war, without end, against terror) are looked at without complacency. As of now it is possible to argue that nuclear power is to the physics world or to nature as capitalism is to economics: both are untameable.

The submission/integration to capital has now reached an unprecedented level: geographical, political, ideological, legal, cultural and religious. In an analysis of the crisis of political leadership in the DRC, Ernest Wamba dia Wamba (2005)[1] pointed out that the state (as fashioned in Africa by capital, from colonial to post-colonial times) appears as genetically coded to be at the service of capital, regardless of geographical borders. Capital has no allegiance and can be truly described as *sans foi ni loi* (faithless and lawless), rewriting rules and laws as it spreads, facilitating its never ending expansion. All and everything is fodder to its insatiable appetite. Could it ever have been emancipatory as envisaged at one point? What can be answered with certainty is that, given how capitalism has evolved, humanity must extract some sort of emancipatory breathing space, while avoiding capitalism's practice of seeking power by any means necessary.

Evil always at the core of capitalism?

The process of definitively extricating ourselves from capitalism's shackles will require applying the following principles: resist its further spread through constant and systematic non violence against all of its manifestations wherever and whenever they are seen and understood. Affirm the mortality of capital by upholding the immortality of the human.

'Unrealistic' some will say. When millions of human beings on earth are faced with living on less than five dollars a day, the only realistic position ought to be to strive to change that as urgently as possible; maybe under the form of 'A Declaration Against Capital as Genocidal', which could signal the beginning of a truth procedure which would render capitalism and its sustaining structures obsolete.

The genocidal nature of capital is hidden from view in great part because the rules for identifying a genocide are written in such a way that capital is safely disconnected from responsibility. In that process basic notions like justice lose their universal integrity because the system has become extremely adept at justifying and rationalising the most unacceptable, the most unjustifiable crimes. The very history of the Second World War Holocaust has preferred to focus on the personalisation of the culprits while, at the same time, trying very hard to erase or downplay corporate responsibility. But even at the level of corporate responsibility, personalising evil by actually naming corporations which benefited from the Holocaust is not very helpful from the perspective of determining with as much precision as possible what is responsible for the inability, reluctance and refusal to identify the most intractable source of evil.

It is obvious why capital, its history and all of the structures which have grown out of it should not be considered as the ultimate source of evil in today's world. Most people, even among those who suffer the most from capital's impact worldwide, are willing to give capital the benefit of the doubt, if only on account of a list of 'positive things' which are associated with capital. Yet, if given a real viable choice, most people would certainly prefer to be able to feed themselves without having to rely on charity.

The convergence and concentration, through and thanks to corporations, of military, economic, financial, political, scientific and religious power in the hands of very few individuals worldwide, is unprecedented. Sometimes it looks as if the Second World War never really ended, and that the fight for world supremacy was reconfigured for the benefit of the one capable of frightening the rest of the world into submission because its military arsenal had the demonstrated capacity to destroy life on earth. This capacity is easy to understand when referring to the nuclear armament industry and militarism, but most advocates of peace on earth are not willing to confront the system which, according to them, sustains both the positive and the negative; because the unstated assumption is that capitalism, by definition, cannot be evil, cannot lead to evil behaviour. Thus, such evil institutions as the Gulag cannot be associated with the US in any way, as Amnesty International found out upon publishing its latest annual report in which it compares the prison networks maintained by the US to the Soviet Gulag. Entertaining such comparisons, thoughts and hypotheses would undermine the basis upon which the triumphal histories of the so-called most advanced nations have been written.

Sometimes the proof that something no longer works takes several failures to be accepted, but what if capital has no way of recognising failure? Capital can no longer impose itself through wars of conquests, even if some continue to think that owning the biggest military machine in history gives them the right to keep reconquering the planet, over and over.

Just recently (20–24 June), Beijing was flexing its muscles in a bid to buy one of the US oil companies (UNOCAL). As if this was not enough of a sign of the changing times, Mr Greenspan, head of the US Federal Reserve Bank, has warned the Bush administration against trying punitive measures against Chinese imports because such a move would not help increase jobs in the US market. However, Greenspan's proposed remedy (among other things, specialising in 'smart jobs' as once advocated by Robert Reich, secretary of labour under the first Clinton administration) will not work because, across the board, from India to China, via Malaysia, Taiwan and South Korea, blue and white collar workers have become smarter and more productive than their US counterparts. Mr Greenspan's thinking is typical of a believer in the global capitalist system, joining hands with the CEOs of IBM, Intel, financiers, bankers, etc, who look at the Chinese market as the ultimate promised land.

Is it bio-technology (life) or thanato-technology (death)?

The US ruling establishment has convinced itself and a great part of the world that its monopoly of weapons of mass destruction is the safest protection against evil, even though the 500-year build-up to this supremacy demonstrates the opposite. And the situation is getting worse. One of the most important indicators of how much more lethal capital has become is the privatisation of the US army and the flow of profits to the corporations. This domination of the military-industrial and prison complex is complemented by domination in the entertainment/sport/ leisure industry (which includes the food industry, the film and advertising industries) whose combined function is to prevent the citizens from thinking, or better to give them the illusion of thinking, under the sedation of the entertainment industry. Thinking outside the box is only meant for profit, for increasing consumption, not for solving social issues. Outside of the box is actually within an already prepared larger box. Empowerment within the pyramidal configuration of the existing power structure cannot help but reproduce that structure when what is called for is its dissolution in favour of the sphere (as beautifully shown by Ayi Kwei Armah in his last novel *KMT: In the House of Life*, Per Ankh, 2002) where the emphasis is away from competition and confrontation and toward cooperation and harmony among people and with nature.

The emphasis on competition has been so severe that it has transformed, for example, the meaning of words like healing. As practised today in the US, the health industry is not about healing, it is much more about how, as the popular phrase goes, to 'make a killing' by looking for (and selling) the miracle cure or the miracle medical technical procedure. The market reigns supreme in the collective and individual minds. Its relentlessness so completely blinds those who should be served that it has acquired a life of its own as though nothing can be done to dampen or control its most destructive features. Simple, common sense understanding of the relationship between one's health and what is eaten and drunk as the best and most effective way of maintaining health is losing credibility, thanks to skilful advertising.

Primitive accumulation is no longer about separating the producers from their means of production, but about stripping human beings of their capacity to think. This divisive mechanism has been so refined, so internalised, that individuals are instinctively more concerned about the survival of the system which is killing them rather than about the survival of their bodies.

Which way forward?

A criminal running away from the crime ends up committing more and more horrendous crimes in order to cover up the previous ones, and so it has been and continues to be with capitalism. Since the crimes have never been acknowledged as such, runaway genocidal sequences continue and are getting worse despite ethics courses being taught in law, business and medical schools, and despite the proliferation of human rights organisations. When the G8 and their formal and informal acolytes vow to fight for Africa and make poverty history it sounded like previous pious vows about abolition. The source of poverty is greed. Capitalism thrives on greed, poverty, violence, warfare and injustice. Why not make capitalism history?

A system which has been genocidal cannot help but seek to reproduce itself through what it perceives as 'having worked' even though the price is becoming less and less acceptable. Given the economic, financial and legal system, conviction will never happen and could only happen if people battle for another world on the basis of principles framed by a higher law, a law which is not framed by the dictates of capital, but by the principles of solidarity, cooperation, justice and peace with all peoples of the planet.

Every year on 6 and 9 August, the Hibakusha (survivors of Hiroshima and Nagasaki), along with nuclear abolitionists and supporters try to remind the world, anxiously, that no one should ever suffer what they went through. Should it not be obvious that the triumphant managers of capitalism and their millions upon millions (generation after generation) of nameless victims are generic Hibakusha, before their time, of a system gone mad?

The anxiety in the voices of the Hibakusha from Hiroshima and Nagasaki comes from wondering what will happen when they die. But one is also encouraged by the inexhaustible fidelity to what is best in humanity, exemplified by Haitians from 1791 to 1804 and through to today, by survivors of the Holocaust battling for Palestinians, by anti-apartheid militants who have refused to cash in on their dues because, as they saw the seamless slide from South African to global apartheid, their conscience called on them to continue in the spirit of those who, in 1791, in Haiti, faced unimaginably worse odds.

Note

1. Wamba dia Wamba, Ernest (2005) 'Le Leadership et la Stabilité Politique en République Démocratique du Congo', *Mbongi a Nsi*, no. 10, 7 juin.

Afterword

Dearest Readers,

You would not be reading these essays if it were not for the efforts of a number of people. Some of whom I may forget inadvertently to mention and thank for their generous support in stimulating the ideas, thoughts which eventually led to these texts for a wider public. The idea of bringing these essays together in a book format was first mentioned by Didac P. Lagarriga, who asked me if he and his organisation, oozebap, could translate and publish (in Spanish) the essays which had appeared in Pambazuka News. For their appearance in Pambazuka News, I must thank its editor, Firoze Manji, and all his colleagues who have created a platform for the voices which either tend to be ignored and/or muffled. On the team I would like to thank, in particular, the editor, Shereen Karmali, for her generous and efficient patience in helping making these essays easier to read and understand.

At times the hardest people to thank are those who have been closest to the process. My most heartfelt thanks to members of the Ota Benga Alliance (www.otabenga.org), Suzie Lyon, Raj Patel, Pauline Wynter, and to Pierre Labossière, the late Father Jean-Juste, Lovinsky Pierre-Antoine and Marilyn Langlois, all connected to the Haiti Action Committee, who acted variously as editors, sounding boards and brainstorming partners about the pertinence of topics.

I am very grateful to Ernest Wamba dia Wamba for his generous critiques and comments, especially about the history of the Democratic Republic of Congo and his constant and salutary reminder that history is made by the masses and not by those who write it. With regard to sequencing of African history I have benefited from ongoing discussions with Ernest Wamba dia Wamba and Michael Neocosmos, as the latter in particular has been reflecting and writing on the subject for the past few years. As director of our partner organisation in Kinshasa, Wamba dia Wamba has made it easier to remain connected to Congolese realities.

Pauline Wynter and I are most thankful to Richard Pithouse and Vashna Jagarnath for organising our visit to Durban in April and May 2008 so that we could meet with members of the Kennedy Road Settlement (Abahlali baseMjondolo – ABM) and their partners of Motala Heights. Shamita Naidoo, also a member of ABM, organised our visit to Motala Heights. During the same visit we met, twice, with S'bu Zikode who, in spite of his reluctance, keeps being re-elected as president of ABM. His thoughts and analysis of the current situation in South Africa deserve a worldwide audience. My deepest thanks for the long-lasting impact all of them, including the ones who are not mentioned, have had on how one should be looking at the histories of the poorest of the poor, the Africans of the continent and beyond.

Although they may not have been aware of it, the students I have been teaching on the graduate programme at the Centro de Estudos Afro-Orientais (of the Federal University of Bahia (UFBA), Salvador, Brazil) did influence how some of the ideas and thoughts developed into arguments. My presence in Brazil (2007–09) was funded through a fellowship from CAPES-Brasil. Among those most responsible for encouraging me to come and teach African history in Brazil, I would like to thank Yusuf Adam, Teresa Cruz e Silva (Eduardo Mondlane University), and Valdimir Zamparoni and Livio Sansone (both at UFBA). From January to August 2007 and from January through June 2008, in Maputo, I had several stimulating discussions with Alexandrino José (Eduardo Mondlane University), whom I had worked with in the History Workshop, under the late Ruth First and the late Aquino de Brangança at the Centro de Estudos Africanos of Eduardo Mondlane University (1980–86). At various times, throughout this period, I was challenged and encouraged to clarify expressions which have found their way into the essays, particularly by Clairemont Moore, Silvia Federici, George Caffentzis and Mamade Kadreebux.

I have benefited from comments, questions, disagreements, doubts at presentations at conferences between 2005 and 2009. I would like to thank collectively all of those who were responsible for inviting me to conferences: Anna Maria Gentili, Henning Melber, Michael West and Bill Martin, Micere Githae Mugo, Arthur Paris, Françoise Vergès, Teresinha Froés Burnham, Wilson

Roberto de Mattos, Paulino de Jesus Francisco Cardoso, Patrícia Schermann, Alyxandra Nunes Gomes, Raquel de Souza, Alain Pascal Kaly.

For always graciously and generously responding to my bibliographic related queries, I would like to thank Colin Darch (University of Cape Town), Phyllis Bishoff University of California, Berkeley) and Karen Fung (Stanford University).

Many thanks to Diamantino Nhampossa, secretary general of the National Union of Peasants of Mozambique (UNAC), for inviting me to the 5th Conference of the Via Campesina (Maputo, 2008). Without his contribution, the piece on the food crisis would certainly not have taken the shape it did. In a follow-up to this meeting, a workshop with the newest members of the international committee of La Via Campesina held in Selinge (Mali, 2009), I was offered one more opportunity to learn and share knowledge outside of the academy.

Last but not least, thanks to Kaidi, Chadi and Pauline Wynter for their permanent spiritual presence and inspiration. Pauline has been the constant, patient and generous sounding-board, primary consulting editor. The piece, on Haiti–Gaza, in particular, owes so much to her that I tried, in vain, to have it co-authored.

Finally, my most grateful thanks to all those I may have forgotten in this list. I am sure the final product will still not satisfy some of the expectations. I promise to do better next time. None of them is responsible for the remaining flaws.

Jacques Depelchin
Salvador, Bahia, Brazil
17 April 2010

Index

Abahlali baseMjondolo (AbM) 43–7, 71

Africa
    and Brazil 33–41
    independence 34

Albright, Madeleine 81

Anan, Kofi 64

Antonian movement 62

Arawaks 30, 54

Aristide, Jean-Bertrand 19, 20–1, 25, 27, 34, 37, 43, 51–2, 62–3

Armah, Ayi Kwei 14n3, 87

Arthus-Bertrand, Yann 13

Badiou, Alain 41n4

Bhaduri, Amit 72

biotechnology 56

Bloch, Marc 15n8

Brazil
    10.639/2003 law 40–1
    and Africa 33–41

Burkina Faso 36

Camatte, Jacques 14n2

capitalism 1–2, 5–6, 57, 81–8

Césaire, Aimé 67–9

China, capitalism 86

Chomsky, Noam 7–8

Cité Soleil, Haiti 18–19, 29

Cohen, Roger 7

Columbus, Christopher 8, 54, 59

crimes against humanity 1–11, 39, 51, 62–3, 66, 73n16

Dallaire, General Roméo 48

Davis, Angela 23–4

Davos 35–6, 42n8, 55

Democratic Republic of Congo (DRC) 24, 48–52, 65

Dupuy, Alex 60

financial crisis 5, 8

food crisis 54–72

France, Taubira law (2001) 9–10, 51, 62–3, 73n16

Francis of Assisi 18, 19

G8 35–6, 55, 83, 88

Gaza 12

Gbadolite 40, 42n13

genocide
    and capitalism 1, 81–8
    Rwanda 52

Greenspan, Alan 86

Gross, Bertram 82

Haiti
    184 protesters 34–5, 36–7
    human rights 23–4
    poverty 18–19, 29–30, 65–7
    slavery overthrow 20–2, 24–5, 60–1

Hallward, Peter 60

Hiroshima/Nagasaki 6, 8, 27, 56, 84, 88

Hodgson, Godfrey 7

human rights 23–4

independence, Africa 34

James, C.L.R. 60

Kashi, Ed 12

Kennedy Road, Durban, South Africa 43, 46

Kissinger, Henry 66

Lovinsky Pierre-Antoine 35, 52

Lumumba, Patrice 25–6, 34, 37, 49–50, 53n5

Machel, Samora 26
Mandela, Nelson 27
Mann, Charles 58
Mbeki, Thabo 21
Motala Heights, South Africa 43, 46
Movement for the Emancipation of
    the Niger Delta (MEND) 16n16
Mozambique 26, 66–7

Naidoo, Shamita 43
Napoleon Bonaparte 10, 23
Niger Delta 11–14
Nkunda, General 48
Nora, Pierre 9, 15n8, 51
nuclear weapons 6–7, 56, 84, 88

Perlman, Fredy 82
poetry 67–9
poverty
    abolishing 31–2
    defining 29–30
    Haiti 18–19, 29–30, 65–7
    South Africa 43–7, 70–2

Quilombo de Palmares 34, 39, 42n11

Rwanda 48, 52

Saint Domingue 15n9, 30, 61–2
Sala-Molins, Louis 10, 15–16n11, 25
Sankara, Thomas 36, 37–40
Santos, Milton 33–4, 37, 40
shame 64–5
Sissako, Abderrahmane 14,
    16–17n23

slavery
    abolition 9–11, 20–5, 51, 68–9
    as crime against humanity 9–10,
        39, 51, 62–3, 66, 73n16
    meaning of 62
South Africa
    end of apartheid 70–1
    and Haiti 18–32
    poverty 43–7, 73n17
Sun City, South Africa 18–19

terror, defining 27–8
TINA syndrome (There Is No
    Alternative to globalisation) 72
Toussaint L'Ouverture 21, 25–6, 63

United Nations
    Conference Against Racism and
        Intolerance 51
    Mission in Haiti (MINUSTAH)
        35, 41n1
United States
    capitalism 86–7
    crimes against humanity 6–9

Vergès, Françoise 67–8
Vita, Kimpa 50, 61–2

Wamba dia Wamba, Ernest 54–5, 84
Winthrop, John 7

Zikode, S'bu 43–7
Zinn, Howard 82
Zuma, Jacob 43
Zumbi 39, 40–1, 42n11

Global History: a View from the South

Samir Amin

978-1-906387-96-9
2010
Paperback £14.95

Responding to the need to take a fresh look at world history, hitherto dominated by Eurocentric ideologues and historians in their attempt to justify the nature and character of modern capitalism, this book looks at the ancient world system and how it influenced the development of the modern world. It also analyses the origin and nature of modern globalisation and the challenges it presents in achieving socialism.

Amin, one of the best-known thinkers of his generation, examines a theme that has been primordial to his contribution to political and economic thought: the question of unequal development. This is a refreshing and creative work that is necessary reading for anyone wanting to understand the real process of history.

I always learn important things when I read Samir Amin. This book is no exception. It is full of original interpretations and is required reading for all who are seriously interested in global history.

Immanuel Wallerstein, Yale University

Africa's Liberation: the Legacy of Nyerere

Edited by Chambi Chachage and Annar Cassam

978-1-906387-71-6
2010
Paperback £12.95

The death in 1999 of Julius Nyerere, Tanzania's first president, left a cavern in the consciousness and conscience of the people of Tanzania and Africa. Nyerere was a Pan-Africanist and internationalist and a giant of the liberation movement.

This book includes contributions from leading commentators, those who fought imperialism alongside Nyerere, members of a younger generation and Nyerere in his own words. Their writings reflect on Nyerere and liberation, the Commonwealth, leadership, economic development, land, human rights and education. Above all, they are a testament to the need to rekindle the fires of African liberation to which Nyerere was deeply committed.